SPRING BOOKS

Ornamental Shrubs

Ornamental Shrubs

Illustrations by
JIŘINA KAPLICKÁ

Text by
JAROSLAV HOFMAN

SPRING BOOKS

Graphic design by W. Ungermann
Translated by Joy Turner-Kadečková
This edition edited by Denis Hardwicke

Designed and produced by ARTIA for
SPRING BOOKS
London • New York • Sydney • Toronto
Hamlyn House, The Centre, Feltham, Middlesex
ISBN 0 600 02882 8

© Artia 1969
Reprinted 1970
Printed in Czechoslovakia by TSNP, Martin
S-3 01 01 51

Introduction

The decorative shrubs illustrated and described in this book represent a fraction of the great variety of such plants which are now available to the keen gardener. Every year new hybrids are being produced by plant-breeders in different parts of the world and the result of their labour becomes ever more evident and adds new delight to our gardens and public parks. Many of the plants described in this book formed, years ago, a basis for the plant-breeder's hybridizing work and in some cases are still used for this purpose.

A great deal has been written about the art of gardening from the days when 'Capability' Brown made whole landscapes, some with the natural informality of lakes and trees, others with spacious formal gardens. That was in the mid-eighteenth century and, while such vast areas are not transformed these days, the art of gardening is still practised even in quite small gardens where the association of plants, their foliage, flowers, autumn colour and decorative berries should all be carefully considered before a planting scheme is undertaken. In a small garden particularly the question of sun and shade must be considered and great effect can be achieved by considering the angle of the sun at different times of the year and trying to allow shafts of sunlight to be thrown on parts of the garden, say in the evening, when the family is there to admire the scene.

It is unwise in a small garden to plant tall evergreens on its south or west sides, particularly if they are on a bank, because they may, when mature, obscure the winter sun from the garden. It must be remembered that during the winter months the sun is comparatively low in the sky and this is the time of the year we need all the sun there is to brighten up the garden. Planting for summer shade, with the sun high in the sky, is another proposition. Much depends upon local conditions and individual requirements, but these points should be borne in mind before planting otherwise in years to come we shall have proved ourselves not to have been very clever.

In many cases a low hedge, say up to 5 or 6 feet in height, is the most suitable to form a screen and one must remember to have borders and paths in reasonable proportions and to avoid straight lines and right angles, where often gentle curves are so much more attractive. On the other hand curves, just for the sake of curves, can look fussy. It is all a question of balance.

It is the same with entrance-gates; one occasionally sees massive pillars surmounted, perhaps, with a pair of stone eagles, and a short approach to a large garage beside a small bungalow. Ludicrous, but presumably it pleases the owner.

A beautiful statue, for which a place is well chosen, for example, beside a pool, can be attractive, but gardens littered with gnomes, storks, brilliantly spotted toadstools and other horrors can be seen too — and in such scenes there is not much artistry.

The siting of individual trees, shrubs or plants with decorative foliage must be done with care. A tree Peony, for instance, is most effective when planted in a bed to itself surrounded by a lawn, or possibly with a background of a wall to protect it from high winds. When planted it may look a little lost at first but it makes quick growth when once established and will develop into a shapely spreading shrub whose foliage is decorative throughout the summer. So it is not only when full of glorious blooms that it is attractive.

Weeping trees, such as a weeping Silver Birch, ornamental Cherry, a dome-shaped Mulberry, are all suitable for a small garden and are particularly effective when viewed from the house across a lawn at some focal point where the sun will make the tree stand out.

When planting a shrub garden do not overcrowd the plants and if a colourful Rhododendron is to be the centre-piece do not let it be overshadowed by some taller tree or shrub, otherwise it will not stand out to its best advantage. Where space permits there is nothing more effective than a bold planting entirely of Rhododendrons or Azaleas to provide a mass of colour during May. In the same way hardy Heathers planted in bold groups will give attractive ground cover throughout the year and if the winter-flowering *Erica carnea* and its varieties are included these will give a most welcome display of colour during the dark months. This winter-flowering Heather and its hybrids such as the deep purple 'King George' and 'Springwood White' will tolerate lime in the soil but many of the hardy Heathers require a lime-free soil as do Rhododendrons and Azaleas.

Colour and background should be considered before planting. For instance, white Delphiniums with their stately spikes against a dark background such as a Yew or Holly-hedge are most effective; yellow Forsythia will stand out well in the early spring sunshine against such a hedge or wall. In the same way a white marble statue should have a dark background and a dark stone or lead figure should stand in a sunny position.

Grey-foliage plants, most of which like a sunny position and a well-drained soil, associate happily with fragrant pinks and other members of the charming Dianthus family. Even when the pinks are not in flower their spiky glaucous 'grass' is attractive. Among the grey-foliage plants are several charming Artemisias. With woolly-white foliage on stems up to 4 feet in height *Artemisia ludoviciana* is a useful plant for the back of a bed or for cutting for flower arrangements. The feathery silver spikes of *A. nutans* attain about half this height. It comes from Sicily and requires a really well-drained soil as it does not like wet winters.

Commonly called Dusty Miller, *A. stelleriana* does well in poor, dry soil, and has finely cut grey leaves on 2-foot stems. The silvery *Anaphalis triplinervis* presents no difficulty in full sun or in dry shade and makes a compact plant about 15 inches high, with densely woolly, silvery-grey leaves and bunches of small off-white flowers. The stem may be cut and dried for winter use. Grey-foliage plants and pinks, even planted in a tub or other container can be most attractive on a roof-garden or for the patio.

Where something larger and fairly spreading is required then *Senecio greyi* will make a handsome shrub up to 4 feet high, with a similar spread. It is evergreen and in the summer has sprays of golden-yellow daisy-like flowers. Shrubs with variegated foliage, Hollies with golden or silver leaves for instance, or the striking evergreen *Elaeagnus pungens* 'Dicksonii' with gold markings on its glossy green leaves are splendid shrubs particularly when seen in winter sunshine. These and a selection of elegant conifers, including golden forms, should not be forgotten when planning a garden of reasonable proportions.

Propagation

Shrubs can be multiplied by various means — seed, division, cuttings or layers, and in some cases by the new technique of air-layering. Shrubs raised from seed are usually sturdy and well rooted but the process is often very slow. Another disadvantage, particularly in the case of species that cross-pollinate easily, is that the seedlings may be variable and not true to type. Such plants must be increased vegetatively, that is by cuttings, division or layers, if the parent plant is to be perpetuated.

Seed can easily be collected from shrubs but it is important to collect it at the right stage of ripeness, usually when it is fully ripe. Sometimes, however, it should be collected before that time, as with plants that scatter their seeds quickly and in the case of certain groups of shrubs, particularly the *Rosaceae* family, Hawthorns, Quince and many rock-garden plants, the reason being that their fully ripe seeds contain substances which may retard germination. In the wild such seeds often lie dormant for some years before germination takes place.

In order to hasten germination, seed which is contained in pods, capsules or other similar receptacles must be spread out in an airy, dry place on sheets of paper, preferably in trays. When thoroughly dry the seed is collected and cleaned by means of a fine sieve. Seed contained in pulpy fruits presents more of a problem. The seed is separated from the pulp by soaking the fruits in warm water and rubbing the mass — it might well be described as a mess — through a sieve. This sieve will need to be somewhat coarser than the one used for dry seeds. Alternatively the pulp can be dried and the seed separated in a dry state.

Germination can be accelerated by soaking seed in tepid water for several hours, or in the case of seed with a very hard skin, for several days. This will cause the seed to swell and in some cases split, or at least soften the covering. When only a small number are to be sown hard-coated seed is sometimes carefully chipped with the aid of a sharp knife. A small piece of the coat is removed on the opposite side to the eye. The seeds of some varieties of Sweet-Pea are treated in this manner.

Hard-coated seeds of many trees and shrubs will germinate more readily if they are stratified, that is, exposed during the winter to frost. Small quantities are sometimes put into a refrigerator for 48 hours or more and then sown in a warm greenhouse, this sudden change of temperature hastening germination. Seeds to be stratified are put into flower-pots and bedded in layers between clean sand, say an inch in depth, and the pots are placed outdoors in the open. A cold-frame without a light is often found to be a convenient place to stand the pots during the winter. Mice may be troublesome so the pots should be covered with fine-mesh netting. In the spring the seed is sown either in a seed-bed in the open ground or in boxes containing seed-compost.

In general, spring is the best time to sow seeds of trees and shrubs, but there are exceptions and seeds of stone-fruit, also Apple and Pear seeds are usually sown in the autumn. Seeds that quickly lose their viability should also be sown as soon as ripe or in the early autumn.

It is most important that seed stored over winter should be kept at an even temperature, a cool, dry cellar being a good place. Different shrubs require different treatment, but, generally speaking, a propagating frame with gentle bottom heat will provide ideal conditions for germination. Such a frame heated by electric soil-warming cables, thermostatically controlled, is a great aid to modern gardening. The days of the hotbed made of manure, straw and the like, with its irritating midges, is a thing of the past.

Before sowing seed always see that the pots or pans are thoroughly clean, otherwise moulds and spores of fungi may prove troublesome in the warmth of the frame. Place a layer of 'crocks' in the bottom of the container and cover this with a thin layer of moss or some rough material to ensure good drainage. Then the container should be filled with seedling-compost to within about half an inch of the rim. The compost may vary somewhat depending on individual requirements; some plants, for instance, need a lime-free compost. Press the compost gently but firmly into the pot with the tips of the fingers and then level the surface before sowing the seed. Do not make the mistake of covering small seeds with too much soil, just a light covering sifted over the top is enough. Then water with a can fitted with a fine rose and place the pots in a frame, either heated or cold, depending on the seeds sown and the time of year. The pots should be covered with paper or shaded from direct sunlight.

The new 'Levington Compost', of which there are seedling and potting mixtures, is a handy means of obtaining a ready-for-use moist compost in neat, clean polythene bags.

The soil must be kept moist, but it is important not to overwater seed that is germinating, and equally so when the seedlings are very small, otherwise they may quickly damp off. For the same reason small seedlings should be ventilated in the frame each morning and if sheets of glass are used as an additional covering to the pots before germination takes place, these must be removed each morning and the condensed moisture removed.

Where only a pot or two of seed is required these can be stood on a shaded window-sill, balcony or verandah and given similar treatment. As soon as germination is evident give the seedlings more air and light, and as they grow more water can be given. When the seedlings are large enough to handle they may be pricked out into boxes or put singly into, say, $2\frac{1}{2}$-inch pots. Often, however, tree and shrub seedlings are left for a year in the original pots — providing they have been thinly sown — and then planted out in nursery beds the following spring.

It is obvious from what has just been said that the process of raising shrubs from seed is slow and involves quite a large amount of work. Where possible, division is much quicker and often more desirable as the parent plant itself is perpetuated. Among the shrubs which can be increased in this manner are Berberis, Spiraeas, Azaleas, hardy Heathers and some dwarf conifers. Division is usually best done in the early spring and the various pieces, complete with roots, should be replanted immediately. If, however, only small pieces are obtainable with not much root these are best put into pots, or planted out in sandy loam in a cold-frame to grow on for a few months. By the autumn they should have become sturdy little specimens.

Layering is another ready method of propagating the parent plant. It occurs naturally with some shrubs, Rhododendrons, for instance, some Cotoneasters and prostrate Junipers. Magnolias are often increased by layering the lower branches in the spring, the procedure being to remove a thin layer of the bark on the underside of the branch for about 6 inches or more and then peg this portion into the soil with two or more layering pegs. If some moist sandy peat is added to the natural soil this should assist root formation. During dry weather this soil should be kept moist. A Magnolia layer will take about 2 years to form sufficient root for it to be severed from the parent plant.

Air-layering is a modern method which has proved most satisfactory with some trees and shrubs. Spring is generally considered the best time to do this work. Briefly the procedure is to make an incision into the stem, selecting a branch about $\frac{1}{4}$ inch thick. Using a sharp knife, treat the cut surface with a hormone growth powder, insert a small wad of moist moss in the cut and then place a handful of clean, moist sphagnum moss around the little branch and cover this with polythene, making a little bundle about 2 to 3 inches in length along the stem. Both ends are sealed with adhesive tape or carefully tied. Some layers so treated may produce roots in 2 or 3 months, but Acers, for instance, may take 12 months or more.

One advantage of this system is that the roots will be visible through the polythene as they develop in the moss. A disadvantage is that the roots are very tender and losses may occur when the layers are first potted up. This is the critical stage in air-layering.

Cuttings are probably the most popular form of propagation. There are various forms: soft cuttings taken from young shoots usually in the spring or early summer, half-ripe cuttings taken in August or September with a heel or slip of the old wood attached, hard-wood cuttings which are usually taken in the autumn and, occasionally, leaf- or bud-cuttings, a method much used commercially for increasing Camellias. Some trees and shrubs may also be propagated by means of root-cuttings, but this method is not often used by amateur gardeners.

Soft-wood and half-ripe cuttings about 4 inches long will root best in a propagating frame where the atmosphere is moist and warm — not hot. Gentle bottom heat will stimulate root growth and this is easily provided by means of electric soil-warming equipment. These cuttings will also root in a shaded cold-frame or under a bell-glass or cloche, but will take longer by these means.

Hard-wood cuttings are taken from leafless shoots in November and inserted in the open ground or in a cold-frame in sandy soil. The cuttings should be about 6 inches in length, about $\frac{1}{4}$ inch thick and of well-ripened young wood. When making the cutting, use a sharp knife and cut immediately below a firm bud at the bottom and just above a bud at the top. When inserted in the soil, about an inch of stem should show above ground level. Be sure to make the soil firm around the cuttings. Leave them in the ground until the following autumn when they may be lifted and planted out in a nursery bed to grow on. In the following spring prune back to one or two buds of the original cutting.

Leaf- or bud-cuttings are best inserted in sharp sand in a closed propagating frame, or under mist-propagation, but this is mainly a commercial proposition carried out on a large scale. Budding and grafting are also methods involving the provision of suitable stock plants and are rarely applied by amateur gardeners.

13

PLATES

Buddleia L.　　　　　　　　　　　　Butterfly　Bush

Named after the English physician and botanist Adam Buddle. A colourful genus comprising about 70 species which grow in the tropical and warmer zones of America, Asia and South Africa. They are mostly shrubs or small trees. Their leaves are opposite, occasionally alternate, with a smooth or serrated blade and stunted stipules. Flowers grow in rich clusters, panicles or heads. They consist of a 4-cornered bell-shaped calyx, a quaternary tubular corolla, 4 stamens and a 2-part seed-vessel with a style and 2 stigmas. The fruit of the Butterfly Bush has the form of an inconspicuous capsule which is usually concealed in the calyx and corolla. Its flowers are fragrant and strongly attract insects, particularly butterflies.

Buddleias are very suitable and attractive in a garden, and flower for a long period, lasting from June to October, a time when many other shrubs have ceased to blossom. The white *B. auriculata,* which comes from South Africa, blooms in the autumn. In the British Isles it can be grown only in the south-west with wall protection. This species is evergreen.

The Butterfly Bush is best planted as a specimen in a small garden and in groups of three at the most in larger gardens. It can also be combined with lower perennials or summer bedding plants to conceal the lower part of the shrub which, especially in the autumn, may be bare. Plants cultivated with Buddleias should not be too highly coloured and care should be taken that their contrasting colours do not disturb the colour scheme.

Buddleias are not fussy; they prefer a light, but by no means poor soil, well-drained, with a neutral to acid reaction. Prune immediately after flowering, by thinning out weak shoots and some of the older wood. A single shrub needs an area of about 3 × 3 feet.

Propagation is done by seed sown under glass or by means of cuttings taken in July or August. Rooted cuttings are grown in pots for another year before being transplanted in a garden.

Buddleia davidii FRANCH.

The most frequently cultivated and extraordinarily variable deciduous species (known also under the name of *B. variabilis*) comes from West China. Its leaves are up to 12 inches long, its flower spikes attaining a length of up to 24 inches. The flower is lilac in colour, the opening of the corolla being orange. The shrub grows to a height of 15 feet or so. The variety *Magnifica* is mauvish-purple and the blossoms of the Pink Pearl are bright pink. *B. alternifolia* Maxim is a graceful deciduous hardy species from China. The leaves are small and the arching branches are covered with fragrant sprays of lilac-coloured flowers in early summer.

16

Campsis LOUR   Trumpet Creeper

The Trumpet Creeper belongs to the *Bignoniaceae,* a large family mostly of tropical plants. Only very few grow also in a milder climate, retaining, however, the character of tropical plants. Two species of this family — the *Bignonia* and the *Campsis* — are vigorous climbers. Due to their similarity they were formerly linked together. The name *Campsis* originated from the Greek 'kamptein' which means to grow crooked and illustrates the climbing character of the plant, as does its common name.

The Trumpet Creeper has deciduous, opposite, pinnately compound leaves with small, sharply serrated leaflets. Its flowers grow in cymes or in panicles. Each bloom consists of a bell-shaped calyx and a tubular infundibular corolla. The seed-vessel ripens in a capsule containing numerous dipterous seeds. The plant flowers from June to September.

It clings by means of aerial roots and climbs up its support to a height of over 30 feet.

The genus comprises 2 species. The first — *C. radicans* — comes from the warmer regions of the United States, the second — *C. grandiflora* — comes from China, but is widely cultivated in Japan. The Chinese species is more tender than the North American one and is consequently cultivated only rarely in Europe, mainly in the Mediterranean region. The hybrid obtained from the two preceding types, *C.* x *tagliabuana* 'Madame Galen', is more resistant. The colour is a rich salmon-red. Campsis are very decorative climbing shrubs suitable for covering fences and walls in warm, sunny districts. They require rich, permeable soil, form deep roots, and stand up well to drought in the autumn. These conditions, together with sufficient warmth, are important for ripening the branches. If the branches mature well there is less likelihood of their being damaged by frost. It is recommended to cover the branches in colder regions. Pruning should be done only in the spring, when older branches are removed in order to encourage young wood on which the flowers are borne.

Propagate in the autumn by taking root-cuttings which are stored in soil during the winter and kept in a mild temperature, or by cuttings in July or August. Hybrids are grafted on the roots of the *C. radicans,* the process being carried out in a glasshouse in the winter.

Campsis radicans (L.) SEEM.   Trumpet Vine

This American species, known also as the Trumpet Honeysuckle, has rich scarlet or orange blooms $2\frac{1}{2}$ to $3\frac{1}{4}$ inches long and $1\frac{1}{2}$ to 2 inches wide. It flowers from July to September. When established this species makes heavy growths and requires additional support to its own aerial roots when growing on a wall, or it may be brought down by summer gales. This plant is also known as *Tecoma radicans.* In the southern part of United States it is considered a harmful weed for it seeds itself freely and will overrun cultivated crops. This does not occur in colder districts where it is prized in gardens.

Chaenomeles LINDL.

Quince

This genus is a small one closely related to *Cydonia,* and often commonly called 'Japonica'. The name *Chaenomeles* comes from the Greek 'cheinein', which means to open gradually, and 'melea' meaning apple. This name obviously describes the properties of the fruit. The name of the other species — *Cydonia* — recalls the town of Kydon in Crete where these small trees have been cultivated since time immemorial.

Quince trees are shrub-like in appearance and grow into 20-foot trees only exceptionally. They are deciduous and quite frequently have somewhat thorny branches. The leaves have serrated or indented edges and short stalks. Characteristic are the sharply serrated stipules. The flowers consist of a 5-sepal calyx and give large petals, the fruits being large, multi-seed pomes.

The flowers are produced either separately or in bunches, their colour usually being some shade of red or orange, and appear either before or shortly after the leaves have developed.

The Quince is propagated by means of seeds or vegetatively. Seeds should be collected shortly before the ripening period. They are planted in the autumn in pots containing well-drained soil and are placed in a cold-frame for the winter. Vegetative propagation is carried out by grafting in June, by layering the branches in the autumn or by means of green cuttings, which are taken from the shrubs in August to September — always with a piece of old wood — and planted in a hotbed or under glass. Cuttings are, however, not an easy method.

The ornamental quinces thrive in well-nourished and well-drained soil with a considerable lime content. If planted in good soil they can withstand a fairly long summer drought and dry soil in general.

They thrive in sun or in partial shade and are fairly slow-growing, forming a freely branched shrub. Pruning should be done in July after the flowering period, but only to remove over-crowded shoots.

Chaenomeles speciosa KOIDZ

Japonica

This shrub grows to a height of almost 7 feet, or considerably more when trained on a warm wall. It has thorny branches, with the exception of the young ones which are smooth and shiny. Its leaves are 1 to 3 inches long, having a sharply serrated edge and a shiny surface. Its scarlet blossoms of 1 to $1\frac{1}{2}$ inches in size grow in groups of 2 to 6. It flowers during March and April. The fruit is oval in shape and about $2\frac{1}{2}$ inches long, yellowish-green to yellow in colour and of a sweet aroma. The shrub comes from Japan.

20

Chaenomeles — *continued*

Quinces are outstanding with their colourful flowers which appear in the early spring or later in May, as well as with their dark, shiny leaves. In the autumn they bear quite large, interesting fruit, usually yellow with red tones, which last long into the winter and even after the leaves have fallen.

Quinces are most suitable for small gardens. They are usually planted in groups comprising one or several types of shrubs and can be suitably combined with quite a number of different shrubs. For example, groups of Quinces with Japanese ornamental Cherry-Trees are very attractive. Such combinations are conspicuous for their colour as well as shape — the bright red or orange-red of the Quinces and the white or pink of the Cherry-Trees. In view of their low growth, Quinces are planted in the foreground, the Cherry-Trees forming the centre of such groups. Quinces and Spiraea, particularly the species that flower early, make an effective combination.

Of the 4 species of Quinces only 2 are frequently cultivated, the *C. japonica* (Dwarf Quince) and the *C. speciosa* ('Japonica'). Both species are shown in the illustrations. A number of hybrids of these two are grown. The best of these are *Atrococcinea* with simple, dark red blossoms (very slow growth), *Cardinalis* with salmon-pink blossoms, *Nivalis* the best white, *Rubra grandiflora* with large red flowers, of spreading habit, and *Rowallane seedling* with large flowing crimson flowers. A third species, *C. sinensis* (Chinese Quince), comes from China. It is a shrub or small tree bearing pale salmon-pink blossoms. Its branches have no thorns and its leaves turn scarlet in the autumn. Its fruit is golden-yellow. It is rather sensitive to low temperatures.

In addition to these species, a hybrid type is often cultivated, namely *C. superba*, the bright orange-scarlet 'Knap Hill Scarlet' being outstanding.

Chaenomeles japonica LDL.   Dwarf Quince

This shrub is about 3 feet high with thorny branches which are felt-like when young. Its wide, egg-shaped, blunt leaves are 1 to 2 inches long and have roughly serrated edges. Its brick-red blossoms are just over an inch wide and grow in clusters of 2 to 3. The shrub flowers in March to April. Its fruit is round, 1 to $1\frac{1}{2}$ inches long, and yellowish-green with reddish spots here and there. The shrub comes from Japan. The form *alpina* is especially desirable, particularly on rock-gardens. It has overhanging branches and vermilion blossoms. The apricot 'Boule de Feu' is a strong-growing variety very suitable for training on a wall.

The 'Japonicas' have been listed in catalogues under various names — *Cydonia japonica, Purus japonica, Cydonia lagenaria* — all of which are now botanically *Chaenomeles speciosa*. Somewhat confusing, but call them what you will they are first-class flowering shrubs.

22

Clematis L. Clematis

The name of this genus is derived from the Greek word 'klema' meaning 'tendril'. It is a genus comprising more than 200 species which are widespread in the mild zones of the Northern and Southern hemispheres. They are perennial plants, semi-shrubs or shrubs, mostly deciduous with opposite, usually compound, leaves. The flowers, appearing either singly or in panicles or cymes, have no petals. The sepals, which are 4 or even 5 to 8 in number, are fairly large and intensely coloured, replacing the corolla both in appearance and function. They have many stamens and frequently flat, sterile stamens as well. The seed is usually provided with a long, plume-like style.

Species may be easily propagated from seed, the seed being sown in pans of well-drained soil in the early spring. Named hybrids are propagated by nurserymen by grafting root stocks of *C. viticella* or the *C. vitalba*. Grafting is carried out in a glasshouse in the winter. A popular method is by rooting cuttings in a warm glasshouse under mist propagation. A simple method of propagation when only a few plants are required is layering. This is done in the summer and the layered branches are covered with a sandy compost. Young Clematis are planted most successfully in the autumn or in the spring.

Clematis are not at all exacting as regards soil. They do well in good, light soil containing some lime and enriched with a small amount of well-rotted manure. Clematis cannot stand direct sunlight on the lower stem and soil around the roots and should not be planted in a south-facing position; western or eastern aspects are most suitable. When planting, choose a place well-protected against the wind by means of either a wall, terrace, or natural formation. It is important to protect the base of the plant. This can be achieved by growing low shrubs round the Clematis. Frequent watering is recommended until the young Clematis is well-established.

Being a climbing plant, the Clematis nearly always needs some form of support. This can take the form of a fence, wall, or trellis. The vigorous varieties are well suited for overgrown old tree-stumps.

In Europe a number of species of Clematis are found in the wild. *C. alpina* (Syn. *Atragene alpina*) grows in the mountains of central and southern Europe. It climbs to about 7 feet with dainty bell-shaped, bluish-mauve flowers. *C. viticella,* with purple to mauve flowers, comes from southern Europe. Central and northern Europe are the home of the white, herbaceous, *C. recta*. Widespread over the whole of Europe is *C. vitalba* known as Traveller's Joy or Old Man's Beard. It is a climbing plant which reaches a height of over 30 feet. It has small, dull white flowers which are grouped in panicles and have a very pleasant scent. This shrub is conspicuous in the autumn with its fluffy seed-heads provided with plume-like styles. *C. flammula* (Sweet Clematis) comes from the Mediterranean regions. It has sweetly fragrant, pure white flowers. Then there are North American species such as the dull white *C. virginiana* or the fragrant purplish *C. crispa* (Marsh Clematis, Curly Clematis). Most widely grown in gardens, however, are the eastern Asiatic species and their splendid hybrids.

Clematis jackmanii THOMAS MOORE

This hybrid between *C. lanuginosa* and *C. viticella* originated in 1860. The climbing variety attains a height of as much as 10 feet, its violet-purple flowers being usually 3 to 4 inches in diameter.

24

Clematis — *continued*

It was in England that varieties of Clematis first found favour in gardens. In 1569, during the reign of Queen Elizabeth I, *C. viticella* was brought to Britain, and it was allegedly in her honour that it acquired the name of Virgin's Bower. This name, together with that of Lady's Bower, has since been applied to all garden varieties of Clematis. In 1573 the beautiful cobalt blue *C. intergrifolia* was brought from southern Europe and a few years later *C. flammula*. In the 18th century these were joined by *C. crispa*, *C. paniculata* and *C. orientalis*. English gardens were mostly enriched in the 19th century with Chinese and Japanese varieties. All these subspecies, which spread from England to the Continent, were quite different from the species previously cultivated. Thus in 1836 great admiration was aroused by the size of the exceptionally beautiful blue *C. patens*. In 1853, a sensation was aroused by the mauve *C. lanuginosa* and in 1865 by the *C. standishi*, now considered to be a variety of *C. patens*, whose mauve blossoms are more than 4 inches in diameter, and the full-blossomed, sweet-smelling *C. fortunei*, named after Robert Fortune, the plant-collector. These and other species of Clematis of eastern origin were used for raising hybrids which are still grown and considerably propagated. This breeding process was started in the 1850's by George Jackman, a nurseryman of Woking in Surrey who selected the *C. lanuginosa* and the *C. viticella* as a basis. On the other hand, Anderson-Henry of Edinburgh crossed *C. patens* and *C. lanuginosa*, Noble of Sunningdale crossed *C. fortunei* and *C. standishi*, and Baker of Bagshot, *C. lanuginosa* and *C. standishi*. They soon achieved surprising results which aroused great admiration at exhibitions in 1855 (Henry), 1863 (Jackman), and 1879 (Noble). In the sixties to the eighties these horticulturists were joined by others, particularly Cripps of Tunbridge Wells, Standish, and Beitch, of Exeter; Lemoine, Simon-Louis, Briolay-Griffon, and Carré of France, and Leichtlin, Croebel, Goos and Koenemann of Wiesbaden, Germany.

Jackman's original Clematis has dark purple flowers. There is also a white form. 'Rubra' is a good red and 'Superba' a dark violet-purple with a wide perianth. Other good hybrids are 'Duchess of Edinburgh' the best double white, 'Gipsy Queen' dark purple, 'Perle d'Azur' a light blue, and the soft heliotrope 'Victoria'.

Hybrids based on *C. lanuginosa* include 'Beauty of Worcester' with mauve single or double flowers with yellow stamens, 'Blue Gem' sky-blue, 'Crimson King', a pinky-red flower with a dark stripe across every petal, 'Lord Neville' with plum-blue flowers and the lilac-coloured 'Nellie Moser'. Well-known varieties obtained from *C. patens* are the mauve 'Etoile de Paris', 'Mrs George Jackman' with satiny white flowers, and 'The President' with dark mauve flowers in summer and again in October. Varieties raised from *C. flammula* include the violet-purple 'Daniel Durondo', 'Duchess of Sutherland' with bright red flowers and pale stripes, and 'King George V', large red blossoms with horizontal stripes.

Clematis viticella L.   Vine Bower

The fragrant, usually purplish-blue flowers of *Clematis viticella* are only 1 to 2 inches in diameter. The Vine Bower comes from southern Europe and western Asia and grows to a height of over 10 feet. The illustration shows the popular hybrid 'Ville de Lyon' with red flowers decorated with darker stripes and noted for their conspicuous stamens with widespread white hairs.

Cornus L.   Dogwood

The name of this shrub comes from the Latin 'cornus' which means horn, a designation obviously derived from the hardness of the wood characterizing all varieties of this genus.

The Dogwoods comprise trees, shrubs and creeping plants (there are two kinds of these, one of which grows in northern Europe and North America — *C. suecica,* and the other in North America only — *C. canadensis*). The genus comprises about 40 species which are to be found mostly in the Northern hemisphere.

The Dogwood is deciduous, rarely evergreen, with opposite, less frequently alternate leaves, and smooth-edged blades. Its quarternary flowers are borne in cymes or heads usually enveloped in bracts, often coloured and consequently wrongly considered petals. The seed-vessel contains 2 seeds and matures into a drupaceous fruit.

From the horticultural point of view *Cornus* may be divided into 3 groups. The first includes shrubs which flower richly in the spring with small, mostly yellow blossoms, usually before the leaves begin to sprout. Included in this group is, for example, the European species known as the *C. mas (*Cornelian Cherry) which in turn has several garden varieties such as *aurea, aurea elegantissima,* and *variegata.* The Cornelian Cherry is conspicuous even in the autumn due to its large red fruits which, unfortunately, soon fall from the shrub. The second group has less conspicuous flowers, usually cream in colour, appearing in the summer. They are attractive in gardens in winter both for their conspicuously coloured branches (for example, red in the case of *C. alba* — Red-barked Dogwood from Siberia), or for their dark blue to black or white fruit. The third group includes only 2 species — *C. florida* from North America and *C. kousa* from Japan. They have 4 large, conspicuous, white or pink bracts in May and June. *C. kousa* has strawberry-like fruits. They are the most decorative and these ornamental shrubs should be planted as single specimens in order to emphasize their beauty. The varieties comprised in the other two groups are usually planted in groups.

With a few exceptions, all the Dogwoods grow best in deep, fertile soil of a moist and heavy nature. They can stand partial or even full shade. *C. mas* grows well in a sunny position in dryish soil containing lime.

The Dogwood is propagated by means of seeds which, however, must be stratified. For this reason winter and summer cuttings, planted in hotbeds, are usually used for propagation purposes. The Dogwood may also be propagated by layering or grafting.

Cornus florida L.   Flowering Dogwood

This shrub is over 15 feet high and is of a tree-like, wide-spreading character. Its bracts are 3 to 6 inches long and white in colour. The shrub flowers in May. The illustration is of the variety 'Rubra' with pinkish to red bracts. During the summer its leaves are fresh green, turning a wonderful red with a purple tint in the autumn. Its fruit is scarlet. It is best to plant the *C. florida* in a sheltered position.

Cotoneaster MEDIK Cotoneaster

The name of this genus comes from the Latin word 'cotonea', which means quince, and 'aster', meaning similar. Thus its name indicates a shrub resembling a quince or a false quince.

Cotoneasters are mostly small, low or moderately tall, upright plants. They are deciduous or evergreen. The leaf surface is usually dark green and shiny, the under part being lighter and very often, at least on the young branches, furry or even hairy. About 50 species are known which grow in the mild zone of Europe, North Africa, Asia, and many in China. Thus they are trees of the Old World which grow neither in America nor in Australia. The calyx of the flowers is trumpet-shaped with 5 short lobes. The petals are upright or spread out, folded in a roof-like manner when the flowers are still in bud. The flower contains 5 stamens and 2 styles. The conspicuous red or black berries are freely borne.

Cotoneasters grow well in dry and light or even rocky soils, thriving particularly in well-drained soil. They like sunlight and do not grow well in deep shade.

They are propagated by means of seeds which are stratified immediately they ripen. They are sown in the spring in the open or under glass. At the beginning of the summer they can be propagated by cuttings of young growths. Rare varieties can be grafted on to Cotoneaster or Hawthorn or Rowan Tree stocks.

Cotoneasters are decorative shrubs, highly popular in gardens. Some are prostrate and are suitable for the rock-garden or for cascading over a low wall.

From the decorative point of view they can be divided into 3 groups according to their growth. The first group includes compact, climbing to creeping shrubs, particularly suitable for rock-

Cotoneaster horizontalis DECNE Rock Cotoneaster

The herring-bone branches of this species are horizontal and spreading. Its leaves are dark green on top and very shiny. The small flowers are pale pink, almost without any stalks, the berries coral-pink and only $\frac{1}{4}$ inch across. In the autumn the leaves turn red to crimson. When planted against a north-or east-facing wall it makes an attractive screen up to 10 feet or more in height.

It is planted on large rock-gardens, its branches spreading over walls and terraces. Other forms of this species are *variegatus* with white leaves suffused red and *perpusillus* with very close growth.

Cotoneaster — *continued*

gardens and walls, which grow to a height of about 20 inches. These include, for example, *C. adpressus* which is prostrate and spreads irregularly. Its wide, egg-shaped leaves are undulating, its small flowers are salmon-pink to red, and its fruit red. The leaves, too, turn red in the autumn. The variety *praecox* attains a height of 20 inches with arching branches. A popular variety is *C. horizontalis*, as illustrated. Mention should be made of *C. dammeri*, an evergreen climbing shrub from West China with white flowers in June less than ½ inch in size. The berries are wax-red.

Other varieties are considerably taller, their number including *C. dielsianus* from central and western China with pale pink flowers and scarlet fruit, *C. divaricatus* with bright red fruit on 6-foot stems and *C. franchetii*, likewise from China and with red fruit. It is a graceful evergreen with grey-green foliage and arching branches up to 12 feet or more in height.

The most numerous group is that comprising the larger shrubs of the species. It includes, for example, *C. multiflorus*, *C. racemiflorus*, *C. frigitus* (Himalayan Cotoneaster), the evergreen *C. pannosus* (Silverleaf Cotoneaster), the evergreen *C. salicifolius* (Willow Leaf Cotoneaster), the *C. simonsii*, and others.

Cotoneasters are the most effective in the autumn when their fruit, mostly red and only in the case of a few varieties black, ripens. As examples of varieties with black fruit can be quoted *C. melanocarpus* from Europe and central Asia, *C. lucidus* from the Atlas Mountains, and *C. acutifolis* from China. The shrubs are usually laden with fruit. In the autumn the leaves of most varieties turn red or dark crimson.

Certain varieties are popular as they retain their leaves during the winter. These include particularly *C. buxifolius*, *C. franchetii*, *C. henryanus*, *C. serotinus*, *C. salicifolius*, and *C. microphyllus*.

Cotoneaster multiflorus BGE.

This shrub comes from West China and attains a height of 10 feet. The flowers are white, its large red berries being round or egg-shaped, its reddish branches growing in an arched, overhanging manner. The cultivated varieties of this species are *calocarpus* with longer, narrower leaves, and *granatensis* from Spain with loose hairy inflorescence and leaves.

These are effective in groups beside paths and lawns as well as on rock-gardens and along fences, walls and terraces.

Crataegus L.   Hawthorn

The name of this shrub originated from the Greek word 'kratos' meaning strength, derived probably from the hardness and toughness of the wood. It is an extraordinarily rich genus, about 90 species growing in Europe and Asia and some 800 in North America. Few are cultivated in gardens, but those that are find extensive use.

All Hawthorns are deciduous shrubs or trees, the majority of them having thorny branches. The blossoms grow in corymbs and only in rare cases individually. They consist of 5-sepal calyx with a 5-petal corolla and 2 to 25 stamens. The fruit is a pome-like drupe with 1 to 5 stones each containing a single seed.

Hawthorns are extremely hardy and easily grown. They do best in a loamy soil, but will thrive quite well in poor and dry soil.

They are increased by seed which, however, as in the case of most stone-fruit trees, must be stratified. They can be propagated by cuttings, or by scallop-budding. Young Hawthorns are often used as a stock for grafting other trees.

Certain varieties of Hawthorn find wide horticultural use, although they are usually planted in large gardens or public parks due to their considerable demands on space. They are planted solitarily or in small groups. They can also be used in avenues, in which case standard trees are used. Hawthorn is very suitable for hedges as it withstands clipping and shaping extraordinarily well. It is not recommended for planting in orchards as it may become a source of pests. Hawthorns are useful as border trees or for planting in protected green zones. They are most effective in May and June when they are laden with white or red blossoms with a strong, almost unpleasant scent. In the autumn they bear bright red, occasionally orange or yellow fruit.

Crataegus oxyacantha L.   English Hawthorn

This shrub or tree is over 15 feet high and widespread in Europe and North America. Its blossoms are white. The illustration shows the variety 'Paulii' *(Coccianea plena)* with full, red blossoms. It is much used in public parks and street avenues. The variety 'Plena' has double, white blossoms, 'Punicea' being the simple, scarlet thorn and 'Rosea' the pink thorn. The variety 'Fructu-luteo' has yellow fruit and most attractive in the autumn is the 'Splendens' variety with its orange to crimson leaves.

Deutzia THUNB.   Deutzia

This shrub was named after J. D. van der Deutz, an Amsterdam alderman, who was a great supporter of the horticulturist Thunberg in his search for new plants. The genus comprises about 50 species mostly from eastern Asia, the Himalayas and Japan.

Deutzias are deciduous with alternate leaves, short petioles and serrated or toothed blades, often smooth-edged at their base. The bark, mostly brown, can often be peeled easily. The flowers grow in panicles or cymes, less frequently individually, usually on the ends of lateral branches. They are mostly white or a pale shade of red or pink. The calyx has 5 sepals and the corolla 5 petals. There are 10 stamens and in rare cases even more. The fruit has the form of 3- to 5-carpel capsules.

Seed is rarely used for propagation. Soft-wood cuttings are taken in June and July or hardwood in October. Root-cuttings may be taken in November to March and are likewise placed in sandy soil in a propagating frame.

Young shrubs are planted from November to the middle of March in deep, well-prepared loamy or sandy soil. Established plants should be top-dressed with leaf mould to encourage growth and ensure an abundance of flowers. They thrive quite well in dryish soil, but not where it dries out completely. Most suitable is a sunny or very slightly shady position. After flowering they are pruned carefully; only old branches spoiling the general shape of the shrubs are removed.

Deutzia scabra 'Plena' REHD.   Rough Deutzia

This variety comes from Japan. It grows to a height of over 8 feet and has serrated leaves over 3 inches long, dull green in colour, and hairy on both sides. Its narrow panicle is about $2\frac{1}{2}$ to 5 inches long and consists of full, white panicles that are pale pink or salmon-pink on the outside. It flowers in June to July. This variety includes the well-known garden type 'Plena', also known as 'Pride of Rochester', which grows in an upright manner with slightly overhanging branches. Its flowers are fully double and consist of narrow white petals with red stripes on the outside. 'Codsall Pink' is a good, tall-growing, double rose-purple hybrid.

Deutzia — *continued*

Deutzias grow upright and their pure white or red flowers are particularly attractive in June although a few varieties flower in May. After the flowering period Deutzias have the appearance of compact, richly-leafed shrubs with light or dark green leaves, according to their type. They are less attractive in the autumn when the leaves of only a few varieties turn a more conspicuous yellow. In most cases, however, their leaves acquire an indefinite, dull yellow hue.

These shrubs are effective singly or in groups. It is recommended, however, to plant them in association with other kinds of trees or shrubs, such as evergreens, shrubs that turn red in the autumn, red-flowering Weigelas or yellow-flowering Barberries, whose leaves also turn bright crimson in the autumn. Deutzias can form an attractive background to a wide rose-bed.

Among the free-flowering Deutzias are 'Kalmiflora' and 'Rosea'. Both these hybrids, the former originating from the *D. purpurascens* x *D. parviflora* and the latter from the *D. gracilis* x *D. purpurascens,* have pink flowers in May but there are several differently coloured forms.

The smaller variety, *D. gracilis* from Japan, begins to flower at the end of May, the flowering period culminating in the middle of June. It is conspicuous for its racemes of pure white flowers, borne on erect stems up to 4 feet high, which usually have a wealth of branches. The flowers are often cut for decoration purposes. It is also suitable for a decorative hedge. Very hardy is *D. parviflora* which attains a height of up to 6 feet and has small white flowers in dense panicles in June. It comes from North China. Most attractive is the Himalayan *D. corymbosa* which has fragrant, snow-white widespread corymbs with conspicuously golden-yellow anthers.

The most frequently planted species is *D. scabra* and its numerous varieties and garden forms.

Deutzia magnifica REHD.   Splendid Deutzia

This variety is the result of a cross between *D. scabra* and *D. vilmorinae*. The shrub grows upright to a height of 8 feet and has strong branches with brown bark. Its leaves are lance-shaped, $1\frac{1}{2}$ to $2\frac{1}{2}$ inches long, and may be almost 6 inches long on young branches. They are finely serrated, rough, bright green on top and greyish-green beneath, and covered with star-shaped hairs. Its double flowers are 1 inch wide, pure white in colour, and grow in panicles in June.

This splendid Deutzia has produced several good varieties including 'Latifolia' with flowers $1\frac{3}{4}$ inches wide, 'Eburnea' with single, bell-shaped flowers in thin panicles and the 'Erecta', with dull white, simple flowers in upright pyramidal panicles.

38

Exochorda LINDL.   Pearl Bush

The name of this shrub is derived from the Greek word 'exo' meaning outer and 'chorda' meaning keel, referring to its keel-shaped fruit. A small genus comprising only 4 species which are widespread in China, Manchuria, Korea and Asia Minor. The Pearl Bush grows to a maximum height of 15 feet and has deciduous leaves with either smooth-edged or serrated, elliptical blades. Its flowers grow in terminal racemes, forming a conspicuous white mass with their wide, shallow, 5-sepal calyxes. The quinary corollas have wide, egg-shaped, shell-like petals (hence, no doubt, the local name). The flowers have 15 to 30 stamens attached by short filaments to the edge of a wide, fleshy receptacle. The seed-vessel has 5 compartments and ripens into a 5-sided, wide, keel-shaped capsule which bursts along its carpellary seams. The seeds are winged.

The Pearl Bush flowers in May. The earliest is the Chinese species *E. racemosa,* while the longest-flowering is *E. x macrantha,* a hybrid raised in France. All varieties are white or cream.

For good growth all require medium heavy, loamy soil, but they will thrive in light, sandy soil if it is not too dry. They do not like thin chalky soils but are not lime haters. They grow well in sunny positions or in partial shade. One shrub requires an area of about 8 × 8 feet.

They are most effective when planted as single specimens in small gardens, or they can also be associated with low types of evergreen shrubs. Very suitable also when grown with Peonies or low-growing Spiraeas. In the latter case it is advisable to choose early or late-flowering varieties. The Pearl Bush is most conspicuous and attractive when in full flower. In detail it is quite remarkable after the ripening of its fruit which, although not conspicuously coloured, attracts attention with its interesting shape.

The Pearl Bush is propagated from seed sown in the early spring under glass in gentle warmth. It can also be propagated from summer cuttings which are rooted in a warm house, but this is not easy. *E. racemosa* is used as the stock for grafting purposes.

Shrubs should be pruned immediately after flowering.

Exochorda racemosa LINDL./REHD.   Pearl Bush

This Pearl Bush is about 10 feet high with white flowers in May. It comes from China and is the one most frequently seen in gardens. Together with the *E. korolkowii* it produced the hybrid *E. x macrantha,* which has longer racemes and is more upright. It is a decorative shrub suitable as a specimen in a sheltered garden. From Turkestan, *E. korolkowii* is well suited for a chalky soil of reasonable depth. It does not like a soil that dries out quickly in a drought. It is vigorous and grows to about 15 feet.

Forsythia VAHL Forsythia

This shrub was named after the English botanist who was the superintendent of Royal Gardens, Kensington, in London (1737—1804). The genus was named by Professor Vahl of Copenhagen and comprises about 7 deciduous species of which one occurs in southern Europe (Albania), the others in East Asia.

Forsythia has opposite smooth-edged or serrated leaves which are sometimes 3-lobed or ternary. Its flowers appear singly or in groups of 1 to 6 in the axils of the preceding year's wood. They consist of a persistent 4-sepal calyx and a 4-petal, bell-shaped corolla which extends into a funnel. They have 2 stamens and a single style bearing 2 stigmas. The fruit consists of a double capsule.

The shrub can be rooted easily by means of summer and winter cuttings which need not be cultivated under glass, but can be planted directly in the garden. They can also be increased easily by layering and from seed.

Its soil requirements are very modest and it fails to thrive only in extremely dry or extremely damp soil. Otherwise it grows well in loam, loam and sand, and in drier positions. When planted in moister places it often grows too vigorously and produces fewer flowers. It can be cultivated in partial shade, but grows better in full sunlight. It is perfectly hardy.

Forsythia grows to a height of about 10 feet; its branches are long and wand-like, and pendulous in some varieties. The shrub is not dense and gives an airy impression which is enhanced by the light brown to greyish-brown colour of its stems. It is not very attractive in winter, its most important decorative characteristic being very early flowering in March and April, the dainty flowers often appearing long before the leaves. Certain varieties *(F. giraldiana* and *F. ovata)* flower as early as February. All varieties of Forsythia are some shade of yellow, ranging from greenish-yellow to golden-yellow. In the spring their branches are laden, and thus they have rightly acquired the name of Golden Bell.

Forsythia intermedia 'Spectabilis' SPAETH

F. intermedia is a hybrid between *F. suspensa* and *F. viridissima*. Its variety known as 'Spectabilis' has 5 to 6 petals of a larger and richer type and it flowers abundantly. They are golden-yellow in colour. The petals are narrow, a typical feature being the curled edges or tips. This shrub flowers somewhat later than other varieties and consequently there is not so much danger of its blossoms being damaged by frost. It is particularly suitable for planting singly or in groups with other shrubs.

42

Forsythia — *continued*

In view of its modest requirements and its conspicuous appearance when laden with flowers in the spring, Forsythia is widely cultivated in parks and gardens. Another reason for its popularity is the fact that it can be cut in the bud stage in February for flowering in a vase in a warm room.

Forsythia is usually planted singly or in small groups. It stands out well when planted in hilly terrain where the individual shrubs can be placed so as to form a cascade. Most advantageous and most attractive, however, is the effect created by combining it with certain other shrubs, especially evergreens. A beautiful effect is created by a Forsythia flowering with dark green Yew trees with other conifers as a background. Equally attractive are groups of Forsythia with Evergreen Berberis, Cotoneasters, Mahonias, underplanted with Daffodils, Scillas, Chinodoxa and other early-flowering bulbs.

Owing to its modest requirements Forsythia is used for many purposes, being planted on rough slopes, in unattractive corners, in front of ugly buildings, and for screening generally. It can be used as an informal hedge.

The Albanian species, *F. europaea* (discovered as late as in 1899 by Baldacci) is rarely planted. The most popular varieties are *F. intermedia* (see illustration) and *F. suspensa* (Weeping or Drooping Forsythia). The latter comes from China and is about 10 feet high with an upright trunk and numerous spreading pendulous branches. It is to be seen in gardens and parks in a number of varieties such as the *sieboldii,* which is suitable for an informal hedge, and *fortunei,* a tall form with vigorous arching branches. The Korean *F. ovata* grows only to a height of about 5 feet and has bright yellow flowers which appear in February. The Chinese *F. giraldiana* is an uncommon species with pale yellow flowers in February, while *F. viridissima* has bright yellow flowers which contrast beautifully with its brilliant green branches. The latter flowers somewhat later and has erect stems up to 8 feet high.

Forsythia intermedia 'Densiflora' KOEHNE

The flowers of this shrub are large and wide, but have relatively short petals which, especially near the end of their flowering time, are somewhat curled. They are considerably lighter in colour than the other varieties, being a pale yellow. This shrub is not so free-flowering as some, but it ranks among the most beautiful of the pale yellow varieties.

F. intermedia is a vigorous hybrid between *F. suspensa* and *F. viridissima* and grows to about 9 feet in height. Two outstanding triploid hybrids raised at the Arnold Arboretum in the United States are the deep canary-yellow 'Beatrix Farrand' with exceptionally large flowers, and 'Arnold Giant' with rich yellow flowers of fine substance. Then there is the low-growing 'Arnold Dwarf' of spreading habit and only about 2 to 3 feet in height.

Fothergilla L.   Fothergilla

This species bears the name of an English physician, botanist and horticulturist who travelled through Japan and later lived for a long time in Stratford, Essex, where he established a botanical garden. The name was given to the shrub by Linné's son, a professor at Uppsala.

It is a small genus; there are only 4 species, all of which are to be found in the coastal and warmer regions of North America. All the shrubs are deciduous and their maximum height is about 7 feet. The wide leaves are usually egg-shaped, shiny green above and lighter beneath, tough, conspicuously veined, short-stemmed, smooth-edged or serrated. The inflorescence is conspicuous in that it has no petals, but only 5 to 7 small sepals. The stamens, with white filaments thickening upwards, bear bright yellow anthers. The fruit is a hairy to bristly capsule with a bell-shaped edge.

Fothergilla requires a moist, peaty, sandy loam of neutral to acid reaction. It thrives best in partial shade. When planted in good soil it can withstand direct sunlight, but often quickly loses its autumn colour. One shrub requires an area of not less than 3 × 3 feet.

It is propagated by means of cuttings which are taken in July and planted in sand in a propagating frame with a sandy-peat base. When the cuttings have taken root they are transferred to pots and overwintered in a cold-frame. It can also be propagated by layering the branches which, however, take root very slowly, sometimes taking as long as 2 years. Even if previously stratified its seeds germinate erratically often 2 to 3 years after sowing.

Fothergilla is a very decorative shrub of neat habit. It stands out well at certain times of the year, the first being in the early spring when it is laden with conspicuous white inflorescences with yellow-tipped stamens. At this period, when gardens are not too colourful, Fothergilla always attracts great attention. It is equally remarkable in the autumn owing to its fiery orange or yellow leaves, particularly *F. major*.

It stands out best when planted singly with an evergreen background.

Fothergilla gardenii MURR

This species is about 3 feet high with upright branches and egg-shaped leaves. The fragrant clusters of white stamens appear in March or April, before the leaves. It comes from Virginia and Georgia. Although it is reasonably hardy, it is recommended to plant it in a sheltered place.

The slow-growing *F. monticola* has an ultimate height of 8 or 9 feet and is somewhat more spreading in habit. When grown in partial shade the foliage is remarkably brilliant in the autumn.

Hibiscus L.   Tree Mallow

The name 'Hibiscus' was used in Ancient Greece (ibiskos) and Rome (hibiscus). Its origin is not clear, but it may be derived from the sacred Egyptian Ibis — a stork which is said to feed on the plant — and 'isko' (similar, popular).

It is a large genus comprising about 150 species, most of which grow widely in tropical regions. Many of the subspecies are very useful shrubs. For example, the annual *H. abelmoschus* from India produces musk-scented seeds (grana moschata, bisma, ambrette) containing ointment essences. it is grown for industrial purposes in Java. Also from India comes the *H. sabdariffa* whose young leaves are used for salads, its pulpy sepals and oil-containing seeds being edible as well. Other species of *Hibiscus* give strong fibres, the so-called rosella-hemp and bast fibres, such as gambo-hemp or Javanese jute.

Only one species, from the Eastern Mediterranean, *H. syriacus* is used as a decorative shrub in gardens. Some of the tender species are cultivated in the warmest regions of Europe or North America, these including *H. rosa-sinensis* (Chinese Hibiscus, Shoe-Black-Plant) with large, funnel-shaped bright red blooms, or the *H. mutabilis* (Cotton-Rose) with large red or white flowers.

In Europe *H. syriacus* only attains a height of up to 10 feet, while in its country of origin it is considered a small tree, growing to perhaps 20 feet. It has deciduous rhombic leaves with short perioles, 2 to 4 inches long, sometimes palmately lobed into 3 lobes with 3 marked veins. Its flowers of 2 to 4 inches in diameter have short stems and are borne individually. They consist of 5 petals which are curled when the bloom is in bud. Its fruits are capsules.

Hibiscus syriacus 'Rubis'

This is a species with single flowers about 3 inches in diameter, red or wine, darker at the centre with darker veins. The leaves are widely lobed, the older ones 3-lobed. It is a frequently cultivated variety.

48

Hibiscus — *continued*

It propagates easily by means of its seeds. Cuttings taken in August with a piece of old wood will root in about 14 days with bottom heat. Garden varieties are usually propagated by layering or grafting. During their first year of growth the grafted plants are cultivated in pots which are kept in a cool glasshouse or frame, or in a place free from frost throughout the winter. They are planted out when they have good roots, usually in the second year after grafting.

Hibiscus requires good garden soil preferably well-drained and not too heavy. It should be planted in warm, reasonably sheltered, sunny places. Its blooms appear on the youngest, terminal growths and consequently pruning must be carried out with due regard to this. In actual fact little or no pruning is required.

There are numerous colourful hybrids which should be more widely planted for they flower from August onwards when most decorative shrubs have finished their display.

Well-known varieties grown in the British Isles include the double white 'Admiral Dewey', the deep blue 'Coeleste' and its double form 'Coeleste Plenus', the double red 'Duc de Brabant', the double white with mauve centre 'Elegantissimus' and the double lilac-red 'Roseus Plenus'. The strong-growing 'Woodbridge', raised in Suffolk, is one of the best single, rich rose-pink hybrids with a deep maroon centre and 'Hamabo' is a splendid pale blush with a crimson blotch at the base of the petals. The flowers are large and single. 'Snowdrift' is a beautiful, early-flowering single white, and 'Blue Bird' is an outstanding, recently introduced, single blue. A good double white of compact habit is 'Jeanne d'Arc' and 'Rev. W. Smith' is a single pure white.

Hibiscus syriacus 'Violaceus Plenus'

A double or semi-double variety, wine-purple in colour and dark mauve to crimson at the centre. The leaves are relatively wide and distinctly 3-lobed.

50

Hydrangea L.   Hydrangea

The name of this plant originated from the Greek words 'hydor' meaning water and 'angeion' meaning vessel, with reference to the fact that the shrub requires adequate water for successful growth. It is known as the Hortensia, the name having been conferred by the discoverer of the shrub in China in 1767, namely the French physician and botanist Filibert Commerson. The Hydrangea was brought to the Royal Botanic Gardens, Kew, for the first time by Sir Joseph Banks in 1789.

The genus comprises about 35 species which grow in North America and East Asia. They are upright, less frequently climbing plants with deciduous, opposite leaves with mostly serrated, rarely lobed blades. The flowers appear in umbels and consist of a 4- to 5-sepal calyx and a corolla of 4 to 5 petals. The number of stamens varies between 8 and 20, the most frequent number being 10. The seed-vessel is surmounted by 4 to 5 short styles. The fruit is a 2- to 5-celled capsule containing numerous small seeds.

The Hydrangea has been cultivated since ancient times in China and Japan. The first shrub of this species to be brought to Great Britain was apparently also a cultivated and not a wild type. Its flowers were red, its umbels composed mainly of sterile flowers. The new shrub aroused great interest at that time with its outstanding beauty. Through cultivation and cross-breeding new forms were produced, but at first the growers were unable to attain much diversity of colour, dull, pinkish-red or pale pink predominating. Indeed the Hydrangea resisted all attempts to improve it for a long time. It was only after the importing of a glowing-red variety from Japan (the 'Rosea' variety) and its cross-breeding with 'Otaksa' that the French horticulturists Lemoine and Mouiller succeeded from 1910 onwards in breeding a large number of new forms differing not only in colour, but also in shape, which surprised visitors to the horticultural exhibition taking place in Paris at the time. Further progress was achieved when it was discovered that the

Hydrangea arborescens L. 'Grandiflora' REHD.

This variety is of North American origin. The shrub grows to a height of about 3 to 5 feet. Its inflorescence is about 7 inches wide without sterile flowers in the species but with them in the form illustrated which is far more decorative. Its flowers are white or pale greenish-white, and are borne in August and September. It is very hardy and will flourish in sun or partial shade. Prune hard each April when the previous year's flowering shoots are cut to within a couple of buds from the base of the annual wood.

Hydrangea — *continued*

Hydrangea reacted strongly to certain chemicals in the soil by a sudden change of colour in its flowers. For example, it was found that iron or ammonia in the soil fostered the growth of blue flower-heads, formerly a very rare phenomenon in this flower.

The Hydrangea is very popular also as a pot plant. Much used for this purpose are the hybrid varieties of *H. macrophylla* Hortensia. They are tender plants which can be cultivated only indoors or in glasshouses during the winter. The advantage of this variety and its different forms lies in the fact that it thrives well in a moist coastal climate with all its special features, including a high salt content in the air. Other varieties can be cultivated in the open, it is true, but it is essential to protect them carefully in the winter, and even then their buds sometimes become frozen, being sensitive to frost. However, there are also varieties which can withstand the British climate well and which may be cultivated without the necessity of taking special precautions. They include, for instance, the shrub-like *H. arborescens* from America, the elegant shrub known as *H. paniculata* from China, the climbing variety *H. petiolaris* from Japan and China, and others.

The Hydrangea is grown in loamy soil with the addition of peat or leaf-mould, or a mixture of leaf-mould and sand. It requires a great deal of water during the growing season and consequently it does better in partial shade rather than in full sun. Most shrub forms of Hydrangea require hard pruning in early spring which results in the growth of strong new shoots and abundant blooms. It is easily propagated by means of cuttings in the spring and inserted in pots containing sandy soil placed under glass, or by means of cuttings taken in August and placed in a cold-frame.

Shrub-type Hydrangeas are usually planted in small groups or as specimens. Pot-grown varieties may be stood in the garden during the summer. They are most effective in window-boxes, tubs or other containers. Very attractive is the self-clinging Climbing Hydrangea, *H. petiolaris,* which soon covers large areas of wall or tall tree trunks by means of its adventitious roots. Decorative and most effective in a woodland garden is the Chinese species *H. sargentiana,* which has large leaves and unusual pale mauve inflorescences.

Hydrangea bretschneideri DIPP.

This species comes from China. Its leaves are 3 to 5 inches long, with serrated blades, pubescent underneath; its slightly arching, off-white inflorescence with purplish stems is 4 to 6 inches in diameter. The flowers are sterile. The calyx sometimes turns a pale purple colour. This tall shrub starts to flower in July. It is a large shrub which attains a height of 10 feet, and requires ample space to develop. To do well it should have a deep rich moist soil.

Kalmia L.   Calico Bush

This genus was named in honour of the Swedish botanist and pupil of Linné, Peter Kalm. It is related to the Ericas and Rhododendrons, resembling them also biologically. It is a small but most decorative genus, mostly from North America (hence its common name of American Laurel) and exceptionally found in West India. Its leaves are evergreen, rarely deciduous, tough, shiny green, arranged alternately, opposite, or in whorls. The flowers grow in terminal or axillary umbels, rarely individually, from the axils of small, thick stipules. The calyx consists of 5 sepals, the wide, bell-shaped corolla of 5 petals containing 10 stamens consisting of thin filaments and anthers covered by the overhanging ends of the petals. The anthers are projected by the stressing of the filaments. The 5-part seed-vessel matures into an inconspicuous capsule.

The earliest to flower is *K. polifolia*, which flowers as early as April, the latest being *K. cuneata* from Carolina, flowering in June or July.

Kalmias come mainly from mild regions and consequently they are not suitable for exposed gardens. They grow happily in the southern and south-western parts of the British Isles, in sunny, protected places facing south or west.

The Calico Bush is not easily propagated from seed. One method is to take summer cuttings and plant them in sandy, light soil in a cold shaded frame. The cuttings should root the following spring, but are not easy. They may be propagated by layering in October.

Like the Rhododendron, the Calico Bush requires a lime-free soil. It grows best in woodland soil or sandy loam with peat. It can withstand sunshine if the soil does not dry out; otherwise it should be planted in shady positions. It seldom exceeds 5 feet in height.

The Kalmias are very decorative due to their dark green, shiny leaves and conspicuous head of flowers and are suitable for growing in smaller gardens. It is recommended to plant them in groups or in association with other ericaceous shrubs, such as Rhododendron, hardy Heather, Skimma, or ground-cover plants such as Pachysandra and Vinca.

Kalmia angustifolia L.   Sheep Laurel

Sheep Laurel comes from the eastern part of the United States. It is a compact shrub which grows to a height of about 2 to 3 feet, having an attractive appearance with regularly spreading, somewhat rigid branches. Its rosy-red flowers appear in May and June. The variety 'Rubra' is deep rosy-red and 'Ovata' is pale pink, the leaves being bluish-grey beneath.

Kerria DC.   Jew's Mallow

The genus *Kerria* was named after the English Botanist William Kerr, a horticulturist at Kew Gardens and later superintendent of the Botanical Garden in Ceylon. He introduced the double form to Kew in 1805. The genus comprises a single species which comes from central and West China, but it has been grown in Japan for centuries. It is from Japan, too, that several varieties and cultivated forms have come. It was cultivated in Europe before 1700, but has been grown more widely since 1860 when Siebold introduced the single-flowered variety.

Kerria was named by Thunberg *Corchorus,* hence the common name Jew's Mallow. It is a small shrub growing to a height of 5 to 7 feet with conspicuous green, wand-like, slender branches. Its deciduous, elongated, egg-shaped leaves are 1 to 2 inches long, bright green on top and lighter green beneath. The cheerful, rich yellow flowers have 5 sepals, 5 petals and numerous stamens. The seed-vessel contains brownish-black seeds.

Due to its moderate size Kerria is popular in small gardens. In parks it is planted in bold groups or in rows in the form of an untrimmed screen.

It requires light, well-drained soil and sunshine, but thrives quite well in semi-shade. The original variety is most often cultivated, but other subspecies are also grown, the most frequently seen being *pleniflora* with golden-yellow double flowers, *aureo-vittata* with green and yellow striped branches, *picta* with white-edged leaves, and *aureo-variegata* with yellow-edged leaves.

Kerria japonica (L.) DC.   Jew's Mallow

The illustration shows this species and a twig of double *pleniflora,* both of which flower in April to May. The hardiest is the single-flowered form. When planted against a north-facing wall (other than in exposed districts) it will reach a height of about 8 feet and provide a bright display in the spring. Propagation is done by means of cuttings taken in August, by hard-wood cuttings about 9 inches long taken in October or November, or by division in the early spring when it is usually easy to remove suckers from established shrubs. Pruning should be done immediately after flowering and consists of cutting out weak growths and shortening the shoots that have just flowered down to strong young shoots.

Lonicera L.   Honeysuckle

This genus was named in honour of the German physician Adam Lonitzer, the author of several botanical works dating from the 16th century, who lived in Frankfurt am Main.

It is a large genus of some 180 species, most of which are widely distributed in the milder zones of the Northern hemisphere.

Honeysuckle has the form of a bushy shrub, or vigorous climber. It is usually deciduous, but there are also evergreen species. The flowers grow in pairs or in threes, sometimes in whorls around the whole stem, from the axils of the leaves. They are quintary, with a tubular, bilabiate corolla, exceptionally regularly 5-lobed. The berries are red, orange or bluish-black to black.

In view of the great variety of types it is difficult to describe a generally applicable character. However, it can be said that most varieties thrive in partial shade. When growing wild they are usually woodland plants. They have no special demands as regards soil and grow well in light, well-drained as well as heavier loamy soils, in neutral and acid soils, and in soils with a considerable lime content. Most varieties are very hardy, the only exceptions being certain climbers from the Mediterranean or from Asia which in the British Isles may be grown successfully only in the warmest and most sheltered gardens.

The Honeysuckle is easily propagated both by seed and by cuttings. In practice it is most frequently propagated vegetatively since this method is quicker and well-rooted plants are obtained in a short time. Summer cuttings are best, taken about 4 inches long in June or July, or half-ripe cuttings can be taken in August to September. Hard-wood winter cuttings can also be used. The cuttings should be inserted in sandy soil in a shaded frame. Layering can be done from August to November.

Lonicera caprifolium L.   European Honeysuckle

This is a European climbing species which reaches a height of up to 20 feet. Its fragrant flowers are white, pinkish or yellow. Its leaves, bluish-green underneath, are pruinose for a long time, later becoming smooth and bare. The shrub thrives well in any reasonable soil and sunshine. It is used to cover fences, walls, pergolas and trellises. It is quite hardy and most decorative when in bloom.

Lonicera — *continued*

Honeysuckle is very suitable for growing on fences, walls, pergolas or on a trellis and it is charming when clothing a cottage porch. In a woodland garden or climbing over an old tree trunk it can be most effective. The native Woodbine of the British Isles, *L. periclymenum,* is a delightful plant which starts to flower in early June and continues to produce its sweetly fragrant flowers off and on until September. They open creamy-white, stained with pink or crimson and turn rich yellow when pollinated, usually by moths at dusk when their fragrance is most powerful. This species is best planted in a wild garden rather than on a house-wall where either of the 2 named forms are more suitable. The variety 'Early Dutch' starts to flower in June, the blooms being deep red outside and rich yellow within, and 'Late Dutch', also known as *L. serotina,* has darker red flowers from July onwards. This is particularly welcome as many climbing plants have finished flowering by mid-or late summer. Both are deliciously fragrant.

Also fragrant is the pink, yellow or white *L. caprifolium* which is sometimes found growing wild in the British Isles, although it is not a native plant. The same can be said of *L. xylosteum,* known as the Fly Honeysuckle, which produces white or yellowish flowers borne in pairs in May and June. Its red fruits are conspicuous in the autumn.

The strong-growing *L. japonica* is not often grown but its variety 'Halliana' does well in sun or shade, bearing small fragrant flowers from June to October. It is evergreen, rather untidy and therefore best planted away from the house, where it could become a nuisance around windows. The flowers open a soft creamy-yellow, fading to the deep ochre which is a peculiarity of the Honeysuckle. The form *aureo-reticulata* has attractive leaves mottled with gold which, being evergreen, are decorative throughout the year both in the garden or when used in floral arrangements.

Lonicera tatarica L.   Tartarian Honeysuckle

This species comes from the southern part of the Soviet Union and Turkestan. It grows to a height of about 10 feet and has small rosy-pink flowers. Its deciduous leaves are bluish-green underneath. Certain forms are popular for the size and colour of their flowers. For example *latifolia* with pink blossoms, *punicea* dark red and *alba* white.

Lonicera — *continued*

The large-flowered *L. tellanniana* makes a great show of rich yellow flowers throughout June and July. They are flushed with red but unfortunately they are not scented. The best yellow Honeysuckle which flowers during the same period is *L. tragophylla*, a vigorous Chinese species which does well in partial shade. Again no scent, but well worth planting. The leaves are 3 to 4 inches long, bronzy-green above and whitish beneath.

The bush Honeysuckles are also delightful but are quite different in appearance from the climbing varieties. The winter-flowering *L. fragrantissima* is a delight with its small creamy-white flowers which fill a room with scent when picked. It is partially evergreen and grows to about 6 feet in height or it may be trained against a wall. The vigorous hybrid *L.* x *purpusii (L. fragrantissima* x *L. standishii)* also has creamy fragrant flowers in winter and is most attractive.

In May and June the Chinese *L. syringantha* has arching sprays bearing tubular, hyacinth-scented, lilac-coloured flowers. It makes a graceful bush about 6 feet high with glaucous-green leaves. Also illustrated is *L. tartarica* with small rosy-red flowers in May and June. It makes an erect shrub up to about 10 feet. There is also a pure white form.

Entirely different and much used for hedging purposes is *L. nitida*, a quick-growing evergreen species which withstands clipping and forms a dense hedge. It is best clipped with a wedge-shaped top otherwise it is liable to be damaged by heavy snow. The variety *L. nitida fartilis* is considered superior, having slightly stiffer branches and larger evergreen leaves. These leaves may drop after transplanting but new ones will soon appear and remain evergreen.

Lonicera syringantha MAX. Lilac Honeysuckle

This is a graceful deciduous shrub which comes from North China and has large bell-shaped, pinkish-white to pinkish-lilac, strongly scented flowers in May and June. The shrub grows to a height of about 6 feet and has slender branches. It is grown chiefly for its fragrance.

Magnolia L.   Magnolia

This is a genus of 80 species named by a French monk, Charles Plumier, in honour of his friend, the botanist Pierre Magnol, director of the botanical garden at Montpellier. Due to its spectacular appearance, wealth of bloom, and rich and interesting foliage it holds a foremost position among decorative shrubs.

The Magnolia is usually a larger shrub or tree; about 35 species grow in North and Central America, East Asia, tropical Asia and in the Himalayas. Its leaves are generally deciduous, only a few varieties having evergreen leaves, and are mostly large and oval in shape with smooth edges. Its blooms are 2 to 8 inches wide, its fruit sometimes forming cone-like formations which may be conspicuously coloured in the autumn. When the follicles burst, the seeds hang from them on long funiculi. The flowers are usually creamy-white, snow-white, or pearl-pink. They often appear early in the spring before the leaves or simultaneously with their development. Such varieties include, for example, *stellata, denudata, kobus,* and *campbellii.* The last named is only suitable for the mildest districts.

The evergreen *M. grandifolia* is the imposing large-leaved shrub frequently seen growing on sunny walls of old houses. Its fragrant creamy-white flowers measure up to 10 inches across and are a splendid sight during the summer months. The form 'Goliath' has even larger blooms and these are produced on somewhat younger plants.

The deciduous Chinese species, *M. wilsonii* has cup-shaped pendent flowers in June and does best in partial shade. The flowers are pure white with conspicuous wine-coloured stamens. For a small garden the most suitable is *M. stellata,* a Japanese species with star-like snow-white flowers in March and April. It is slow-growing and its maximum height and spread are about 15 feet.

Magnolias require good, loamy, well-drained soil containing leaf-mould and peat. As many of them flower in early spring it is advisable to plant them in protected places, particularly where they are shaded from the morning sun.

Young shrubs can be transplanted easily, the best time for this being in April, at the beginning of May, or in October. Large shrubs do not transplant readily. It is not easy to propagate Magnolias by seed. However, if this method is used the seed should be sown as soon as it is ripe and stood in a cold-frame. Germination may take from 12 to 18 months, but will not be hastened by artificial heat. Cuttings taken in June or July about 4 inches long and with a heel will root in pure sand in a temperature of about 70° F. Layering branches take about 2 years to root and they should be pegged down in early spring. Grafting is carried out in July and August with some varieties.

Magnolia soulangeana SOUL.   Soulangeana Magnolia

This variety was named after Soulange-Bodin, of Fromont, near Paris, where it flowered for the first time in 1826. It is a chance hybrid of *M. denudata* and *M. liliflora.* The former has wide, cup-shaped, pure white fragrant blooms and the latter has purple blooms, white within. The hybrid, *M.* x *soulangeana* has large blooms ranging from mauve to pink and pearl-pink. The varieties cultivated most frequently in gardens attain a height of 17 to 20 feet with blossoms 4 inches wide. The first flowers appear in April before the leaves and continue until late May, when the tree-like shrub is in leaf.

Paeonia L.   Peony

This genus was named after the Greek god of medicine, Paieon, referred to by Homer in Iliad.

'However, the god Paieon put healing medicine on his wound, with which he healed him who was not intended to die.'

This medicine which, in the poem, Paieon gives to Hades, the god of the underworld, was apparently a Peony. The curative properties of this plant were referred to in ancient times by both Theophrastus and Pliny. Throughout the Middle Ages it was considered to have therapeutic properties and was consequently widely cultivated in the herbal gardens of monasteries and in private gardens, finding wide application also in folk medicine. Today we know that the curative properties of the Peony are not very outstanding. It contains starch, a quantity of tannin and only traces of alkaloids. Its curative reputation is based rather on the fact that it was used in the folk cult and that certain of its parts, particularly its seeds, were worn as amulets affording protection against illness and disease, particularly in Switzerland, Denmark, and Portugal. The mild toxic effects of the Peony (alkaloids) are recalled in the German folk name by which the Peony is known, 'Giftrose', which means poisonous rose, although it is more commonly known there as 'Pfingstrose' or Whitsun rose.

The Peony usually takes the form of a hardy herbaceous plant, but its 33 species include a very small number of Tree Peonies. It has large, alternate leaves, and white, yellow and red blooms. Its fruits are follicles. Apart from a single species which grows in North America, Peonies are widely distributed in Europe and Asia.

The oldest species to be cultivated in Europe is *P. officinalis* which comes from southern Europe, including Albania. It is up to 24 inches high, and has single, attractive ruby-red flowers with conspicuous filaments bearing small, golden-yellow anthers. In gardens this wild variety is mainly cultivated in its double forms in which the filaments are transformed into petals. The double varieties are white and pink to red. Other species come from the Mediterranean, namely *peregrina* and *mascula* with dark red flowers.

Paeonia suffruticosa ANDR. var. *alba crispiflora*

This variety is a Tree Peony which grows to a height of about 3 feet. Its flowers may be as much as 10 inches across, pure snow-white at first, their centres later turning pink. It flowers in June and is very hardy.

68

Paeonia — *continued*

The European Peonies did not form the basis for later development and breeding. Indeed, it can be said that these local European varieties were at first completely overlooked. Development started with the import of the white-flowered Chinese *P. lactiflora* which became the basis of the largest number of double Peonies of various colours, ranging from the most common bright glowing shades over snow-white and yellow to various hues of red, pink, crimson and purple.

The diversity of Chinese Peonies is far greater than that of European varieties, consequently affording great opportunities to the plant breeder. The Peony has been cultivated in Chinese and Japanese gardens for ages; nowhere has it enjoyed such interest, popularity and fame as in those two countries. Whole districts, indeed whole regions concerned themselves with the growing of Peonies for the market, this activity being considered not as a mere profession, but as a predilection enjoying the protection of the gods. Even in ancient Chinese literature there are references to Peonies, with legends and poems praising the beauty of these plants. Hybrids also acquired names in full accord with the tastes of the Orient, such as 'Sun in the Forest', 'The First Desire of the Lying Virgin', 'My Friend Pleased Me in the Garden', 'Water Sleeping in the Shade of the Moon', 'A Maiden Offering Her Bosom', 'My Robe is no Longer Snowy White, but Torn, the Son of Heaven Left Some Pink Blood on it'.

The first Japanese varieties were imported in 1844 by Siebold, a Dutch nurseryman of Leyden, and were propagated and distributed, but did not seem to survive for any length of time.

The so-called Chinese and Japanese Peonies are generally speaking 2 groups of varieties, the former being double, free-flowering forms, and the latter simple varieties with flat, band-like yellow to orange-yellow stamens.

More conspicuous are the Tree Peonies with their large and splendid blooms. The first to be imported was known as the Moutan, later renamed *suffruticosa*, from which many fine varieties have been raised.

Tree Peonies require deep, moist loam or loam and sand. When planting choose a sunny place facing south and protected against the wind. In summer droughts mulch with peat and water the plants well. In the winter they should be top-dressed with well-rotted manure which also affords protection to the roots against frost. In severe weather it is also recommended to use brushwood over the surface soil but leave the parts of the shrubs above ground uncovered. The

Paeonia suffruticosa ANDR. 'Beauty of Tokyo'

A Tree Peony with velvety crimson blooms as much as 10 inches in diameter.

reason for this is that Peonies come into growth early in the spring and if the leaf buds were given such protection they would be speeded up even further, resulting in frost damage of the leaf buds or even of the branches.

Wild varieties of Peony can easily be propagated by means of seeds which usually ripen in adequate numbers.

Seed should be sown in pans of sandy soil in September and placed in a cold-frame. The seedlings are likely to differ considerably in various ways. Hybrids can be increased by division of the roots in early spring and these will, of course, be true to type.

Tree Peonies are increased by grafting, usually on to root-stocks of *P. lactiflora* or *P. officinalis*. This is done in April and the grafted plants are stood in pots in a cool house. When grafted plants are put out into open ground they should be planted at a sufficient depth to ensure that the union of the stock and the scion is below soil level. This will encourage roots to develop from the scion — that is, the grafted portion — to give a stronger, long-lived plant.

Peonies flower in May to June and are usually laden with large, handsome blooms. Both herbaceous and Tree Peonies lend themselves well to cutting. To ensure the flowers last well in water, they should be cut when they are only just showing colour and are quite firm.

The most frequently cultivated Tree Peony is *suffruticosa* which has wide, egg-shaped leaflets in large, 3- to 5- lobed leaves, grey and smooth or only slightly hairy underneath. The sessile leaves are about 4 to 10 inches long. The flowers appear singly on the branches and are 6 inches or more in diameter. The shrub grows to a height of about 7 feet. There is a large number of double varieties of different colours cultivated in gardens, which have been raised by European and American firms, as well as hybrids from China and Japan. Hybrids include the pink 'Arashiyama' , 'Beni-Kirin' orange-red, 'Fuka-jishi' ('God of Lions') crimson, 'Jeanne d'Arc' salmon-pink, 'Athlete' white with lilac on the outer part, and 'Black Bird' dark purple. Elegant but less frequently grown are the Chinese *delavayi,* a tree variety reaching a height of about 4 feet with pinnated leaves 6 to 10 inches in diameter. Another is *lutea,* also a shrub, which attains a height of 5 feet. Its attractive, fragrant, yellow flowers are about 2 to 4 inches in diameter. They are not very numerous and consequently are often concealed among the fern-like leaves.

Paeonia suffruticosa ANDR. 'Belle de Nancy'

A Tree Peony with salmon-pink blooms about 12 inches in diameter. The shrub flowers in June and grows to a height of about 2 to 3 feet.

Philadelphus L.   Mock Orange

This genus is interesting for its very name. Its scientific name recalls the Egyptian King Ptole-maius Philadelphus (about 250 B.C.) who married his sister (the Greek word 'philein' means to love and 'adelphos' child of the same parents). Its English name, Mock Orange, is used also in the United States. Apart from this, it is also sometimes called 'Syringa', which is the botanical name for Lilac. In French, too, the Philadelphus is called 'Seringat'. In some other European languages, such as German, Dutch and Czech, the name *Philadelphus* is connected with quite a different tree, namely with the East Asian 'Jasmin' (Czech 'Jasmín', German 'Falscher Jasmin', Dutch 'Boerenjasmin'), again an entirely different plant, known botanically as *Jasminum*.

The genus *Philadelphus* comprises 40 species and very many garden forms. The majority of species grow widely in East Asia, less widely in North America and somewhat rarely in South Europe and the Caucasus.

All have deciduous leaves, their flowers mostly being white, occasionally pale pink or reddish. They form terminal racemes comprising sometimes a number, at other times only a few, large blossoms. The fruit is in the form of a 4-part capsule.

Philadelphus gordonianus LINDL. var. *columbianus* REHD.

This shrub is about 12 feet high with young, regularly spaced branches, yellow or grey non-peeling bark, and white flowers 1 to 2 inches in diameter in June and July. It comes from North American Idaho and British Columbia.

74

Philadelphus — *continued*

The Mock Orange can be propagated from seed, but it is rather a lengthy business. For this reason vegetative propagation is more popular. Autumn hard-wood cuttings about 12 inches long can be put into sandy soil in the open, or in June and July half-ripened nodal cuttings about 4 inches long are put in pure sand in a propagating frame with bottom heat, in medium heavy loamy soil. They require a sunny or only a slightly shady position, and are perfectly hardy under normal winter conditions. To ensure good growth and a wealth of bloom the older wood should be thinned out immediately after flowering.

The Mock Orange is very suitable for small gardens. Planted as single specimens those varieties with arching branches are seen at their best. The taller, erect-growing varieties should have lower-growing shrubs or hardy perennial plants around them. To enliven the autumn colour in the garden it is useful to plant perennials which flower at that period in front of Mock Orange shrubs.

It was M. Lemoine, the French horticulturist of Nancy, who was one of the first to play an important role in the cultivation and hybridizing of these decorative shrubs. He crossed *P. microphyllus* from North America with *coronarius* from Europe, and the splendid offspring was named *P. lemoinei* — a very fragrant, pure white shrub, about 6 to 8 feet high. This has given rise to a number of hybrids — 'Avalanche' with a mass of small, fragrant white flowers on arching branches, the dwarf 'Boule d'Argent', and the double 'Enchantment' among others. Although Mock Orange hybrids are not climbing shrubs, many may be trained to grow on walls or pergolas, where they are very effective.

Philadelphus nivalis JAQUES

This is a hybrid between *pubescens* and *coronarius* which was known before 1840. The bark is brown and can usually be peeled; the leaves are hairy underneath. Its white flowers are borne in sparse racemes and are about 1 to 1½ inches in diameter. Derived from this hybrid is the double form known as *plenus*.

Prunus L.   Almond, Cherry, Peach, Plum

Some 200 species are known, as well as innumerable named cultivated forms, most of which are ornamental-flowering or fruit-bearing trees. They are widely distributed in the temperate zones of the Northern hemisphere. Systematically this large genus is complicated, usually being divided into several groups: *Cerasus* (Cherry), *Padus* (Bird Cherry), *Laurocerasus* (Common Laurel), *Amygdalus* (Almond), *Armeniaca* (Apricot) and *Persica* (Peach).

From the horticultural point of view the genus is divided into shrub and tree varieties. Many are used for garden purposes, some of them being particularly popular like the hybrid Japanese ornamental cherries; they include *P. serrulata* hybrids, the large double rosy-pink 'Kanzan' and 'Shirofugen' with pink buds opening to double white blossom, and many other varieties. The Bird Cherry, *P. padus*, a native of Europe and North Asia, and *P. serotina* with dark brown aromatic bark from North America are also cultivated. Varieties of *Laurocerasus*, the Common Laurel, are useful evergreens to form a wind break. Unless they are cut regularly they develop into wide-spreading shrubs 20 feet or more in height.

The various members of the genus *Prunus* are not difficult so far as soil conditions are concerned. They can withstand a dry climate and usually prefer a sunny position. The Flowering Cherries are perfect as avenues. Only a few varieties require rich, moist soil to ensure good growth; *P. padus*, for instance. They can be propagated by means of seeds which, however, must be stratified. Named varieties are budded or grafted on the appropriate stocks by nurserymen.

Prunus tenella BATSCH   Dwarf Russian Almond

This low-growing shrub is also known under the name of *Amygdalus nana* and *Prunus nana*. It comes from western Asia, eastern Siberia and south-east Europe. It is a small shrub attaining a height of 3 to 5 feet and flowering in March to April. Its flowers are up to an inch across and are borne singly or in pairs along the whole length of the branches. They are usually pink in colour, although there is a white form 'Alba', and 'Gessleriana' (also known as 'Fire Hill') is rosy-crimson.

The Dwarf Russian Almond is a very suitable shrub for planting in small gardens or on a rock-garden particularly if associated with decorative grasses or low-growing evergreens.

78

Pyracantha ROEM   Firethorn

The name of this shrub originated from the Greek word 'pyr' meaning fire and 'akanthos' meaning thorn. The first part of the name obviously refers to the fiery colour of the fruit, the second to the thorny character of the majority of the varieties. The genus has 6 species widely spread in Central China, the Himalayas, and one in southern Europe.

They are large shrubs, some attaining a height of 18 feet, with alternate evergreen leaves. Their flowers form umbels. The fruit is a small red, orange or yellow pome with a persistent calyx containing 5 small nuts.

It is propagated by means of seeds sown in the autumn. Cuttings about 4 inches long may be taken during the summer of the current year's growth with a heel and placed in a propagating frame. Autumn hard-wood cuttings should be put in a cold-frame. Seedlings and rooted cuttings should be put in pots and grown on for at least a year.

Mature shrubs are difficult to transplant, unless lifted very carefully with a block of soil around the roots. Young plants should be clipped and abundantly watered. In the coastal areas of Europe Firethorns are quite hardy, but may be damaged by frost in the continental regions. They like fresh loam, or loam and sandy soils and a sunny position.

They are very decorative when in flower, being conspicuous for their large creamy-white umbels; in the autumn they are brilliant with colourful berries. They are frequently grown against house walls and are valuable for use as hedges as they are thorny and withstand cutting well. They are used with effect in roadside planting. In severe frost they may lose their leaves, but will soon produce fresh leaves in the spring.

Popular varieties include *P. angustifolia* with orange-yellow berries and narrow leaves, *P. atalantioides* with crimson berries, *P. rogersiana*, orange-red and its variety 'Flava' with bright yellow fruit. The most commonly cultivated, and particularly popular for its exceptional hardiness, is *P. coccinea* 'Lalandii'.

Pyracantha coccinea ROEM   Scarlet Firethorn

The Scarlet Firethorn comes from Italy and western Asia. It flowers in June, having creamy-white flowers in dense umbels. It attains a height of about 10 feet, or up to 20 feet against a wall. Its brilliant red berries ripen in September to October. The most popular variety is 'Lalandii' with bright orange-red fruit and long, slender branches.

80

Rhododendron L.   Rhododendron

The name of this shrub comes from the Greek words 'rhodos' which means rose and 'dendron' meaning tree. Included in this varied genus are also the so-called Azaleas whose name was derived from the Greek word 'azaleos' meaning dry. Unlike the Rhododendrons, most of which are evergreen, Azaleas are mainly deciduous.

This is an extraordinarily large genus comprising as many as 750 species of which some 500 are estimated to grow in western China alone. About 60 species grow in East China and Japan, and about 30 in North America, mostly on the territory of the United States and Canada. A single species is found in northern Europe; eastern Europe produces 4 species, and 3 species grow in central Europe. At present only a single species is recorded in Australia, the waxy-red *R. lochae* from the Queensland Mountains.

Rhododendrons are usually large shrubs sometimes reaching tree size, (some Chinese species attain a height of 85 feet in the Himalayas). They have single, deciduous (the Azalea) or evergreen, smooth-edged (rarely serrated) leaves which are usually tough and leathery, being slightly or much darker and shiny on their upper side and lighter, dull and sometimes hairy underneath. Their flowers are borne in racemes, individually, or in groups. They usually consist of a quinary calyx which, however, sometimes has 6 to 10 sepals. The bell-shaped or wheel-shaped corolla has a marked tube, consisting of 5, rarely 6 to 10, sometimes deeply forked petals. The flowers are never completely regular and contain 5 to 10, sometimes more, stamens, a 5-to 10-part seed-vessel with a slender style, and a wide stigma. The fruits are egg-shaped capsules containing numerous small seeds.

Rhododendron luteum SWEET   Yellow Azalea

This variety is also known under the names of *Azalea pontica* and *Rhododendron flavum*. It comes from East Europe, the Caucasus and Asia Minor. It has deciduous leaves and grows to a height of as much as 12 feet, with fairly sparse branches. Its bright yellow flowers are borne in May in small racemes on the ends of the branches and are sweetly scented. The sepals as well as the leaves are bristled. The autumn colouring of the foliage is remarkably beautiful. Being very hardy, it is often used as a stock for the grafting of hybrids. It is one of the originators of the Ghent Azaleas and has given rise to many popular hybrids.

Rhododendron — *continued*

Although Rhododendrons grow widely over enormous territories, their soil requirements are very uniform. Apart from a few exceptions, *R. hirsutum*, the 'Alpine Rose' and its close relative *R. ferrugineum,* they cannot stand lime in the soil. In gardens, sufficient acidity is ensured by adding peat to the soil, which also helps to retain moisture. Another characteristic of Rhododendrons is their large moisture requirements which must not, however, be overdone. They like a moist cool soil — not waterlogged — and a moist atmosphere. For this reason they thrive best in coastal regions of the mild zone in which, in western Scotland, Ireland and Cornwall, there is ample rainfall and the variation in daily and yearly temperatures is small and they are not threatened by frost. Hardy as they are, the blooms may be damaged by inclement weather.

Where Rhododendrons are to be grown successfully in less favourable conditions it is necessary to endeavour to create somewhat similar conditions. Most suitable are west-and north-facing sites. It is also important to ensure protection against the prevailing wind. Some varieties can withstand direct sunlight, their susceptibility to the sun depending on the moisture content of the soil, but most Rhododendrons grow best in partial shade. Where possible plant them among established trees. In the winter a top-dressing of peat or leaf-mould will benefit the shrubs. This covering maintains moisture in the soil as well as giving additional protection against frost to the roots. During long summer droughts watering may be necessary.

As far as soil is concerned, Rhododendrons should be planted in medium heavy lime-free loam. Heavy soil is made lighter by adding sand and peat. Very wet soil must be drained. Soil

Rhododendron vaseyi GRAY   Pinkshell Azalea

This American species from North Carolina grows to a height of from 8 to 15 feet. Its pale pink or reddish flowers are only about an inch in diameter. It is a deciduous shrub, hardy in mild coastal regions, but requiring protection in less favoured areas. This very decorative shrub flowers in April and May, before its leaves have fully developed. Its leaves turn red in the autumn. It can be propagated easily from seeds. The variety was named after G. S. Vasey who discovered it in 1878.

Rhododendron — *continued*

with a large humus content is most suitable. On poor soil add well-rotted farmyard manure in moderation. Artificial manures must be used sparingly; bone meal, being slow acting, is sometimes added to the soil when planting.

Rhododendrons can be propagated from seed, but this method does not usually yield plants true to type, particularly if the seeds are collected where a large number of varieties are growing. It is practically impossible to propagate named hybrids true to colour from seed. Consequently, Rhododendrons are usually propagated vegetatively, in spite of the fact that with some varieties the procedure is by no means easy.

Cuttings are taken from mature plants in July to August and planted in a cold-frame or glasshouse. Alpine varieties can be rooted reasonably well, but large-leaved varieties are not easy. Layering may be done in August or September and sometimes takes as long as 2 years. Hybrids are propagated by grafting in February; the stock generally used by nurserymen is *R. ponticum,* the now common mauve species.

The Rhododendron is one of the most outstanding decorative shrubs and perhaps the most beautiful of all. It is also a genus which has been more successfully hybridized in Europe (and particularly in England), than in the East where the growing of plants has been practiced since time immemorial.

Fossilized remains of Rhododendrons have been found in Europe and in the United States and have been estimated to be 50 million years old. Although we come across references to the Rhododendron dating from the time of Xenophont (400 B.C.), garden varieties of the shrub

Rhododendron yedoense MAX.   Korean Azalea

This deciduous shrub comes from Korea and Japan, being widely cultivated in both countries. It is also known under the name of *Rhododendron poukhanense* var. *yedoense* or var. *yodogawa*. It grows to a height of only about 3 to 5 feet and has purplish-lilac, strongly scented flowers in April. The variety 'Yodogawa' has semi-double flowers and is semi-deciduous.

86

originated in Europe at a much later date. In Great Britain the first reference to the Rhododendron was made by Parkinson in 1629. The first species to be imported to the British Isles was *R. hirsutum* which was brought from the Alps in 1656. In 1680, *R. indicum,* a red-to scarlet-flowered Azalea whose numerous varieties are grown in pots today, was brought to Holland from China. Soon afterwards this species disappeared. In 1808 Anderson introduced *R. simsii* which flowered for the first time in the garden of James Vere in Kensington; it reached France from there in 1825. Before that, however, other varieties were sent to the British Isles, the first *R. nudiflorum* coming from America in 1734, *R. viscosum* in 1736, others later from Asia via Gibraltar (in 1763 *R. ponticum* and directly from Asia in 1780 *R. dauricum,* in 1793 *R. luteum,* in 1796 *R. chrysanthum*). However, at the end of the 18th century only about 12 species were cultivated in English gardens.

Rhododendrons began to be more widely introduced in the first half of the 19th century. As early as 1803 *R. caucasicum* reached Great Britain from Asia and *R. minus* from America, followed by the outstanding *R. catawbiense* from North America in 1809, *R. arboreum* from India in 1815, *R. molle* from China in 1824, *R. zeylanicum* from Ceylon in 1832, and later *R. campanulatum* and *R. barbatum* from the Himalayas. In 1844 Fortune sent several new eastern species such as *R. obtusum.* At the same period, numerous hybrids began to appear in the British Isles and in western Europe.

The first European hybrid came into being as a cross between the *R. nudiflorum* and *R. ponticum* which originated before 1814 and was grown in the collection of the Royal Botanic Garden,

Rhododendron schlippenbachii MAX.   Royal Azalea

The species was named after Baron von Schlippenbach, a naval officer and traveller. The shrub attains a height of as much as 15 feet. It comes from Korea, Manchuria and Japan. Its large, deciduous leaves grow in a whorl, usually in fives. It flowers in clusters of strongly scented pale pink to rosy-purple blooms in April and May. In the autumn its leaves turn orange to red. It is not reliably hardy and consequently it should not be grown without winter protection except in warm coastal regions. Otherwise a sheltered position is essential.

Rhododendron — *continued*

Edinburgh under the name of *Azaleodendron*. Round about 1810 Michael Waterer began to concern himself with the breeding of Rhododendrons, cross-breeding the North American *R. maximum* and *R. catawbiense,* and later crossing the progeny with the Asian *R. arboreum*. In 1835 *R. caucasicum* was crossed with *R. arboreum* by Waterer, the resulting early-flowering red hybrid being named 'Nobleanum'. His son, Anthony Waterer, continued these breeding activities and in less than a quarter of a century 1,500 new hybrids were raised in the nursery at Knaphill.

The arrival of 2 species *R. molle* from Ghana and *R. japonicum* from Japan was an important occurrence. These, together with the very fragrant yellow-flowered *R. luteum*, gave rise to a large number of hybrids. The first to gain merit for these hybrids is supposed to be a baker from Ghent, named Mortier, who worked on them early in the 19th century. He raised a large number of hybrids which were outstanding particularly for their bright yellow and orange shades and fiery-red colours. These hybrids found great popularity especially in Great Britain where further cross-breeding continued. Great attention was also devoted to these varieties by Belgian horticulturists, in particular van Cassel and Louis and Alexander Verschaffelt, and later Jean Verschaffelt and Louis van Houtte. The Azalea growers of Ghent were also responsible for the origin of a number of hybrids known under the collective name of *R. gandevensis*, having orange, pink, red, and purple flowers. They originated as the result of cross-breeding *R. luteum* with *R. mortürii*, the latter being a hybrid between *R. calendulaceum* and *R. nudiflorum*. Further crossing of the Ghent Rhododendron (Azalea) with *R. molle* resulted in numerous types with mostly double flowers of the most diverse colours.

Rhododendron praecox CARR.   Early Rhododendron

This is a hybrid between *R. ciliatum* and *R. dauricum*. Its regularly-arranged, semi-evergreen leaves are 1 to 2 inches long, sparsely bristled and dark green on top. The wide, funnel-shaped flowers are pinkish-purple, and up to $1\frac{1}{2}$ inches wide. The shrub flowers very early, some years showing colour in February. It is quite hardy, but the flowers are susceptible to frost damage.

Rhododendron — *continued*

Great merit for the raising of the 'Ghent Azaleas' is due, in the first place, to Louis van Houtte and Vuylstecke who, in the 60s, put new hybrids on the market with exquisite, sometimes almost too bright, colours. Later on great success was achieved by D. A. Koster in Boskoop in Holland who succeeded in crossing *R. molle* with *R. japonicum* with such good results that the new race proved hardy; it is also possible to bring them into flower early under glass — a fact which has made them of considerable commercial value.

Two trends can be traced in the plant-breeders' work carried out in the 19th century. On the Continent, attention was devoted rather to Azaleas, usually to dwarf varieties intended for growing in pots and less frequently to Azaleas intended for cultivation in the open. Contrary to this, the trend in the British Isles was the breeding of evergreen Rhododendrons. This was obviously due to the extraordinarily suitable climate. Breeders and nurserymen endeavoured, in the first place, to attain beautiful and effective colours or flowers of remarkable size and form. In Europe this target was supplemented by still another, namely production varieties tolerant of low temperatures.

In the 80s of last century the well-known Dresden horticulturist Seidel finally came to the conclusion that English varieties could not be acclimatized in continental Europe, only a few of such varieties being hardy enough to withstand the severe Central European winter. Horticulturists there tried first of all to cultivate a frost-resistant type based on hardy varieties, but only succeeded in obtaining a few such resistant varieties. In consequence, growers embarked

Rhododendron catawbiense MICHX. Catawba Rhododendron

This compact evergreen shrub grows to a height of 10 feet. Originally it came from Virginia and Georgia (being named after the town of Catawba) and grows abundantly in the Alleghan Mountains. Its leaves, up to 6 inches long, are lance-shaped with blunt ends. Its lilac-purple flowers, spotted with olive green, are over 2 inches wide. The shrub flowers in May and June and has given rise to numerous hardy hybrids.

on a different trend. They began to cross-breed naturally resistant varieties such as the North American *R. catawbiense* and Caucasian *R. smirnowii,* and obtained hardy hybrids. Later on these were again re-crossed with *R. catawbiense,* giving rise to a large number of large-flowered varieties which are often to be seen in Central European parks.

An outstanding hardy hybrid is known as 'Cunningham's White'. It is considered to be a cross between *R. caucasicum,* which is rarely grown in gardens and *R. ponticum album.* It is a good variety for town gardens and does quite well when grown in a large tub. It provides a good stock for grafting a large number of varieties.

A special colourful group comprises hybrids obtained from *R. obtusum.* These hybrids are usually called 'Kurume Azaleas', after the Japanese town of their origin. Brilliant varieties of these Kurume azaleas are bright crimson 'Hinodegiri', clear pink 'Hinomanyo' and the crimson-purple 'Hatsugiri'. Arends crossed these Kurume Azaleas with *R. mucronatum* var. *noordtianum* and obtained very hardy and exquisitely richly flowering varieties with evergreen leaves and large, lilac-coloured, pink, bright red to crimson flowers. These hybrids are usually known under a collective name in honour of their originator, namely *Azalea arendsii.*

It is only comparatively recently that breeders have endeavoured to obtain varieties outstanding for the elegant shape of their flowers rather than for their size and colour. Popularity is being gained by hybrids with trumpet-like flowers of rich texture. This trend is particularly obvious in the United States where Rhododendrons have been increasing in popularity since the beginning of the century.

Rhododendron smirnowii TRAUTV. Smirnow Rhododendron

A hardy species from the south-west Caucasus, is a slow-growing shrub up to 7 feet high. Its felted evergreen leaves, 3 to 6 inches long, are grey beneath, later turning a rusty colour. Its dark pink to rosy-purple flowers appear in June and are 2 to 3 inches in diameter.

94

Rhododendron — *continued*

It is only natural that such a beautiful and diverse genus has given rise to numerous specialist societies. The oldest of these is the Rhododendron Association which published the Rhododendron Yearbook from 1946 (published by the Royal Horticultural Society from 1954 under the title of the 'Rhododendron and Camelia Yearbook'). Other outstanding associations are the German 'Rhododendron Gessellschaft' and 'The American Rhododendron Society'.

Rhododendrons are admirably suitable for use in parks and woodland gardens. They are most effective when planted in bold groups. Proof of this can be seen in the European Alps, in the Carpathians and in the Caucasian mountains, where the local species set the slopes afire with their glorious blood-red flowers.

Rhododendrons are also suitable for borders when planted in groups, either large or small. They stand out well when planted near walls, terraces or a background of conifers. In small gardens offering only little space these shrubs may be planted singly. Rhododendrons are very attractive when planted in an island bed surrounded by well-kept lawns; they are also very effective near streams and pools.

Some compact, low-growing varieties are particularly well-suited for rock-gardens. For example, *R. repens* with bell-shaped scarlet flowers, *R. hirsutum* with pinkish-red flowers, *R. ferrugineum* (the well-known rosy-crimson Alpen Rose), *R. ledoides* a fragrant pinkish-white, and the stunted *R. intricatum* with lilac flowers.

Rhododendron 'Cunningham's White'

This is a vigorous hybrid growing to a height of up to 17 feet. It has dark green, shiny leaves, and mostly white flowers. It is very hardy and consequently frequently planted in continental Europe. It flowers in April and has been much used by plant-breeders for many years.

Ribes L.   Currant

The name *Ribes* was derived from the Arabic word 'ribas' or 'riwas' meaning sour fruit or rhubarb. It obviously refers to the sharp-flavoured fruit of the majority of varieties of this species. The genus comprises about 150 species which grow widely in the temperate zone of the Northern hemisphere, occurring in the Southern hemisphere only in a part of South America along the Andes as far as southern Patagonia. All varieties of the Currant are of bush-type, some being thorny and some not. Their leaves are simple, their flowers growing singly or in racemes, followed by juicy berries with the fruiting varieties.

Currant bushes can easily be propagated from seed; it is quicker, however, to take hardwood cuttings during the autumn. These should be about 12 inches long and of the current year's growth. Plant them in the open, preferably in sandy soil.

Of the large number of different varieties, only a few are planted in gardens for decorative purposes in spite of the fact that they are undemanding shrubs and thrive well in soils of medium quality and often in drier soil, both in sun and partial shade.

Among the varieties most frequently grown in gardens is the tree-flowering *R. sanguineum* which can be seen in the illustration. Another popular variety is *R. odoratum* the 'Golden Currant' from North America. This has bright yellow flowers and a refreshing clove scent. Another widely cultivated variety is the European *R. alpinum* with inconspicuous greenish-yellow flowers. It does well in shade and makes a useful hedge.

Currant bushes are, with a few exceptions, very suitable for small gardens. They are not spectacular when in flower, but with their shapely appearance and dense foliage they are useful for screening or hedging purposes, both when clipped or when allowed to grow freely.

Ribes sanguineum PURSH.   Flowering Currant

This North American species is remarkable when in flower, being freely laden with racemes of rich flowers in March and April. It grows to a height of up to 10 feet. Some of its forms are particularly interesting, such as 'Albescens' with white flowers tinted pink, 'Atro-rubens' with dark red flowers, 'Splendens' a dark blood-red, and salmon-pink 'Carne-um'. There is also a double-flowered form. Named varieties include the clear pink 'China Rose', 'Pulborough Scarlet' which makes a good tall shrub and the bushy 'King Edward VII' with long, deep crimson racemes. Flowering currants do not require regular pruning but weak growths should be thinned out immediately after flowering.

Rosa L.   Rose

The name is derived from the Greek word 'rhodos' and from the Latin 'rosa'. The genus comprises about 150 species and innumerable hybrids. In the wild they are to be found over a vast area of the Northern hemisphere from Siberia to the Himalayas, in North America, and as far south as Mexico, in Europe and North Africa. The majority of the Rose species are shrub-like in appearance, although some are vigorous climbers. They are deciduous and only in rare cases evergreen. Blooms of the wild Rose are usually borne singly or in clusters at the ends of short branches. They consist of 5, occasionally 4 petals which in the case of many garden hybrids are considerably multiplied. They have numerous stamens and pistils enclosed in a cup which ripens when fertilized into a fleshy, often colourful fruit called a hep or hip, which contains small pips. Some Roses are thornless, but the majority have thorns on their stems varying from hooked barbs to small prickles.

The Rose is the oldest cultivated garden shrub. The earliest representation of the Rose in Europe is thought to be in the frescoes at Kressus on the island of Crete. Sargon, King of Babylon, around 2700 B.C., sent to Akkad 'two species of fig trees, vines, Rose trees and other plants'. The Island of Rhodes had a Rose on its coins and probably acquired its name from the much cherished plant.

The Romans had a great love of the Rose and it was widely cultivated in gardens at that period. It has been popular throughout the ages but it is impossible to determine when definite attempts were made to produce hybrids of different species. The Rose cross-breeds itself readily and many natural mutations have occurred which have caused much interest and delight for many generations.

The Chinese *R. odorata,* or Tea Rose, widely cultivated in China, was brought to England in 1810. This proved to be a very hardy species and was crossed with *R. chinensis,* the China or Monthly Rose, which had already been established in Europe for quite a number of years. The Bourbon group of Roses is said to have originated on the Ile de Bourbon from a natural cross between *R. chinensis* and *R. damascena,* the Damask Rose. This pink hybrid appeared in

Hybrid Tea Rose 'Bettina'

Raised by Meilland, of Cap d'Antibes, France in 1953. Its parentage is 'Peace' x ('Mme. Joseph Perraud' x 'Demain'). Of vigorous growth, it bears large double, fragrant salmon-orange flowers with bronze markings. The foliage is dark glossy green but is susceptible to mildew in some gardens. It is free-flowering particularly in the autumn and the blooms last well when out.

Rosa — *continued*

1817 and many good hybrids have been obtained from the progeny, such as the famous cream and blush-pink 'Souvenir de la Maison', whose fragrance first filled the air in 1843. This Rose is usually at its best in the autumn.

One of the earliest Hybrid Tea Roses was the highly fragrant, free-flowering, silvery-rose 'La France' with pale lilac shading which was raised by Pierre Guillot in 1867. In its day it was a magnificent Rose, but has lost its vigour over the years. Hybrid Tea Roses are grown in vast numbers these days — almost every garden has a few — and their large, conical blooms are borne erect on the tips of long stems. They are produced singly and not in clusters as with the modern Floribunda varieties. They usually start to bloom in June and many of them produce a splendid autumn display as well. The colour range of modern hybrids is remarkable and some have intense fragrance.

Rose-breeders are now paying considerable attention to producing hybrids that are resistant to mildew and other fungus diseases with the result that many Roses now have sturdy, glossy foliage which is handsome and in many cases free from disease.

The modern Floribunda Roses, which used to be known as hybrid Polyanthas, appear to be superseding the Hybrid Teas in popularity. The reasons for this are their remarkable hardiness, long period of flowering and in many cases immunity from disease.

In the early 1920s Poulsen in Denmark started crossing Polyantha Roses with Hybrid Teas and later such names as 'Elsa Poulsen' 'Karen Poulsen' and 'Kirsten Poulsen' became well known. Kordes in Holstein was busy breeding this type of Rose and in 1933 he introduced the large carmine-red 'Eva', a hybrid *R. moschata,* which he later used with great success for breeding purposes. By crossing descendants of *R. moschata* and *R. multiflora* Kordes obtained varieties which showed considerable resistance to fungus diseases.

A great deal of work has also been in progress in recent years in the United States of America where an outstanding large-flowered type known as 'Floribunda Grandiflora' has been developed. The Irish firm of McGredy as well as Alex Dickson have played their part in the development of the modern Floribunda and Hybrid Tea Roses.

Floribunda Rose 'Mary'

This shrub from 'Orange Triumph' was introduced by D. Qualm in 1948. The parent plant was raised by Wilhelm Kordes in North Germany in 1938 ('Eva' x 'Solarium'). 'Mary' is similar in habit with orange-yellow to red flowers borne in trusses. They are slightly fragrant and up to 2 inches in diameter. It makes a good bushy plant.

Rosa — *continued*

Miniature Roses have become fashionable in the United States where some 150 named varieties are grown by enthusiasts. Some such as 'Oakington Ruby' and the crimson 'Tom Thumb' have been grown on English rock-gardens for a great many years, also the little double pink *R. pumila* which makes a neat bush about 18 inches high. These are reasonably hardy but some of the modern hybrids are not happy in severe winters.

The little Garnette Roses which are in shades of red, pink, coral and yellow are long-lasting and most decorative for florists' posies. They are useful for growing under glass either in a warm or cold house and can also be grown in the open so long as the position is not too exposed.

The cultivation of old varieties of Roses has increased considerably in recent years due partly to the great interest now taken in the art of floral arrangement to which they lend themselves so handsomely. One of the finest collections of such Roses is to be seen in La Roseraie de l'Hay-les-Roses, near Paris, and in the Parc de Bagatelle, Paris, will be found the modern Hybrid Tea and Floribunda Roses which are grown there and judged each June by an international jury of rosarians. The Queen Mary Rose Garden, Regent's Park, London, the Parc de la Grange, Geneva, and Messrs. Jackson and Perkins Rose Garden at Newark, New York, are all justly famous for their splendid collections of Roses.

Cultivation

Roses are a permanent feature in a garden and once planted they resent transplanting. Therefore the soil should be thoroughly dug to a depth of 18 inches, if the sub-soil allows, but this sub-soil should not be brought to the surface, but broken up so as to improve the drainage and to assist deep rooting. Roses like a rich soil so work into the ground farmyard or horse manure; garden compost, leaf-mould or peat are all beneficial. This preparatory work should be done at least three or four weeks before planting to allow the soil to settle. Peat and leaf-mould are particularly useful on light soil as they help to retain moisture around the roots.

Planting is usually done from the end of October until the end of March, so long as the weather and ground conditions are favourable. However, now that Rose trees are available at garden centres growing in containers it is possible to fill gaps in a rose-bed even during the summer as

Rosa multiflora THUNB.

This species from Japan was introduced to France about 1860. It has also been found growing in the wild in Korea. It is a strong climber, up to 20 feet high, bearing single white flowers in large corymbs. The French Rose-breeders of Lyon raised a host of seedlings from this species and, selecting the best, eventually produced what were then known as Poly-Pompon Roses.

Rosa — *continued*

by this method the roots are not unduly disturbed. Rose trees planted from containers will, of course, require watering during dry periods until they have become established.

When planting Rose trees lifted from the open ground the roots should be spread out as far as possible and the soil made firm around them. When the job is completed the union of the scion and the stock should be just below the surface soil. Bush Roses should be planted about 18 to 24 inches apart, depending upon the vigour of the variety. Rose species vary considerably in height and spread so they require ample space to develop. They should be planted not less than 4 feet apart and many will require considerably more space for their long arching branches.

Established Rose trees should be given a good mulch with manure or compost each spring before growth starts. There are also special Rose fertilizers which are useful to stimulate bud development during the growing season. Some can be used in liquid form and it is important to use them according to the maker's instructions. Quick-acting fertilizers should not be given when the soil is dry, but it is quite safe if the soil is well-watered. In any case they should not be given after the second half of July or soft growth will be encouraged in the autumn and this is to be avoided.

Pruning

Roses that start making growth early in the New Year, that is mainly shrub species and climbing varieties, are best pruned in December or January. Summer-flowering rambler Roses should have the old wood cut out in September after they have flowered and the new shoots tied in. Established Hybrid Teas are pruned hard in March or the beginning of April and Floribunda varieties are pruned at the same time but not nearly so drastically. Roses are pruned every year when weak growth should also be cut out and with bush Roses inward-growing branches should be cut back so that an open shapely bush is formed.

Late frost may cause damage to tender young shoots which have come into growth after pruning, or frost immediately after pruning may cause the stem to die back at the tip. In such cases all that can be done is to prune again to the next eye lower down the stem.

Rosa rugosa THUNB.

This species, sometimes called the Ramanas Rose, was introduced from Japan and Korea about 1845. It is also found in North China. It makes an erect shrub up to 8 feet in height with large, deep purplish-pink, single, fragrant flowers in June and July. It produces suckers freely and will form a dense hedge. The leaves are dark green and shiny and turn golden-yellow in the autumn. Its large orange-red hips are most decorative in the autumn and are often used for making preserves. This plant is widely used as stock for budding purposes. There are double and single forms as well as a white variety.

Rubus L.   Bramble

The name of this shrub comes from the Latin word 'ruber' meaning red, referring to the most frequent colour of its fruit. Botanically it is a genus of considerable size which is estimated to comprise 400 species. However, this figure must be considered only approximate, because Brambles interbreed freely, producing natural hybrids.

All are small shrubs, semi-shrubs or herbaceous plants, with deciduous or evergreen leaves with perennial or biennial stems. The stems are often erect, arching or even creeping, sometimes provided with thorns, and bear alternately-placed simple or more often palmate or ternary leaves. The seeds ripen in small drupelets which are joined on a common receptacle, forming a fruit of the well-known blackberry type.

Most Brambles will grow in poorish woodland soil. They can withstand shade, but under such conditions usually produce fewer flowers and fruit.

They can be propagated by means of seeds sown in pans in the spring and placed in a cold-frame. It is easier to propagate them, however, by means of stem-or root-cuttings taken in July or August and placed in a cold-frame.

As decorative shrubs, Brambles are mainly useful as low-growing creeping or climbing plants. They can be used to cover walls, terraces, fences, or pergolas. Other types may be used as ground cover plants. There are also varieties which may be planted as specimen shrubs or in groups. The varieties used to cover the ground include, for example, the North American *R. hispidus*. Among the climbing varieties are *R. henryi*, and *R. flagellifolius*, both of which are evergreen; the prostrate varieties include *R. irenaeus* and the bushy, somewhat straggling varieties include *R. chroosepalus* and *R. lambertianus*. The shrubby varieties include *R. odoratus R. parviflorus*, *R. crataegifolius*, *R. spectabilis*, and others. The first variety to be cultivated before 1770 was probably the arching *R. linkianus*, which is conspicuous for its double white flowers of up to 1 inch in diameter. A remarkable characteristic of some varieties is the special and conspicuous colouring of their branches. Outstanding among these 'whitewashed' branches are *R. cockburnianus,* and *R. lasiostylus* with blue branches. A splendid new hybrid *(R. deliciosus* x *R. trilobus)* raised in recent years in England is named 'Tridel'. It has glistening white flowers up to 3 inches across with prominent yellow stamens.

Rubus odoratus L.

This is a deciduous, upright vigorous shrub from North America. It is conspicuous for its sweet-smelling and handsome, purple flowers about 1 to 2 inches in diameter which are borne in the summer. Its leaves are hairy and its fruit red. The shrub grows to a height of about 8 feet. It is thornless. There is also a white form known as 'Albus' or 'Albidus'.

Spiraea L.   Spiraea

The name of this shrub comes from the Greek word 'speira' meaning wreath, thread, or ringlet, that is something twisted or curled. Some authors attribute another meaning to the Greek word, namely 'wounded' or 'someone with an open wound', this supposedly referring to the fruit which consists of dry follicles conspicuous for their widely cleft appearance on ripening.

Spiraea is a decorative genus comprising about 80 species as well as numerous hybrids and garden forms. It grows in the temperate zone of the Northern hemisphere, in the northern part of Asia and as far west as the Himalayas. It is also found in Japan and western America. Only a few are native European plants.

All the varieties of Spiraea are shrubs with alternate, deciduous, simple leaves with indented or serrated — occasionally even smooth — edges, cone-shaped to egg-shaped. The flowers have 5 sepals, 5 petals, and 5 pistils. The fruit is a follicle which splits along its inner seam. The flowers are borne in umbel-like racemes.

It is propagated by half-ripe wood-cuttings taken in July or August, placed in a cold-frame. Hard-wood cuttings are taken in the autumn and put in a cold-frame for the winter. Certain varieties which do not root easily are propagated by means of cuttings taken from plants specially grown in a glasshouse. For example, *S. thunbergii*, *S. arguta*, and *S. prunifolia*. Some may be increased by division in the autumn or early spring.

Spiraeas are not difficult as regards soil; some varieties even thrive in poor, dry soil. They can be planted in shady positions, but usually grow better in sunny, fairly open places; under such conditions they usually flower profusely. In the case of early-flowering varieties pruning should be done immediately after the flowering period. Old and dried branches should always be removed. In late-flowering varieties, pruning should be done in the winter or early spring, but in any case while the plant is dormant.

Spiraea arguta ZAB.   Garland Spiraea

This is a beautiful spring-flowering hybrid (*S. thunbergii* x *S. multiflora*). It has thin branches with fine, slender, shoots; its lanceolate leaves are about 1 to $1\frac{1}{2}$ inches long and sharply serrated. The shrub reaches a height of about 7 feet. Its snow-white flowers appear at the end of April and the beginning of May. It grows well in dry, light soil but appreciates a liberal top-dressing of leaf-mould or well-rotted manure during the growing season. It associates well with Forsythia and Chaenomeles, and is very effective when planted against a dark background of conifer or a yew hedge.

Spiraea — *continued*

Spiraeas are colourful shrubs. They have a very attractive appearance and are well-formed, regular, and often widespreading; some varieties have arching branches while others are erect. Most varieties are free-flowering with wand-like, often long, branches richly covered with blooms. These are usually white, yellowish or cream, although quite a large number of varieties have a pink, pinkish-mauve or dark red head of flower. Their flowering period is extended, different varieties flowering at different times from April to September. From the decorative point of view Spiraeas are divided into 2 groups according to their flowering period. Flowers appear on the earliest varieties before the opening of the leaves or at the same time. These early kinds include *S. thunbergii* which comes from China and has pure white flowers in April, *S. prunifolia* 'Plena' double-flowered variety which comes from Korea, Japan and Formosa, the tender *S. cantoniensis* which comes from China and Japan and its double variety known as 'Lanceata' with lanceolate leaves, the freely-branched and somewhat rigid *S. nipponica* with dark green leaves, very shiny on their upper surface and white flowers up to $\frac{1}{2}$ inch in diameter, *S. veitchii* which comes from China and displays handsome, softly pubescent cream inflorences, *S. hypericifolia*, a southern European and central Asian variety whose white flowers have very conspicuous stamens, and *S. trilobata* which comes from North China and Siberia and has 3-lobed leaves and rich umbels of white flowers. Included in this spring and early summer group are certain hybrid varieties which are widely cultivated. For example *S. vanhouttei*, which originated by crossing *S. cantoniensis* and *S. trilobata* and has clusters of pure white flowers, and *S.* x *arguta* (known as 'Foam of May') which is *S. thunbergi* x *S. multiflora*.

The second group comprises varieties which blossom from about the middle of June to September. While the early varieties mostly have white flowers, the later-flowering types are usually pink or red. The Japanese *S. japonica* has pale to salmon-pink flowers from June to July. It is widely grown in gardens, including 'Fortunei' and 'Macrophylla' varieties, the last named

Spiraea salicifolia L.   Willow Spiraea

This species comes originally from Central Europe, although it is found over a wide area reaching as far as East Asia. The shrub attains a height of 5 or 6 feet and has tough, erect branches which lend it a somewhat severe appearance. Its lanceolate leaves are about 3 inches long, sharply serrated in their upper part, bright green on their upper surface and light green with bluish tinge beneath. Its salmon-pink clusters are borne in erect pyramidal panicles about 4 inches long. The shrub flowers from June to July.

It can be planted effectively either singly or in groups and is often used in hedges.

being grown mainly for its autumn colour. Also later-flowering are the erect *S. salicifolia* (see illustration), *S. menziesii* which comes from North America (from Alaska to Oregon) and has small purplish-pink flowers clustered in long, narrow panicles, *S. latifolia* (the Pink Meadow Spiraea, Meadowsweet or Queen-of-the-Meadows) also from North America, with pinkish-white flowers notable for their long red stamens, clustering in wide pyramids, *S. alba* from North America (the Meadowsweet or Meadow Spiraea) with long leaves and white panicles. A hybrid obtained from *S. japonica* x *S. albiflora* named *S.* x *bumalda*, has dark pink or dark salmon-pink flowers which grow in wide cymes; it attains a height of about 30 inches and flowers well into August. Its most popular varieties are 'Anthony Waterer' with stiff leaves and crimson flowers and 'Froebeli' which is taller, has wider leaves, and flowers somewhat earlier. Summer-flowering Spiraeas also include the North American *S. douglasii*, a large vigorous shrub with terminal spikes of dark red flowers, and *S. tomentosa*, with dark pink flowers which grow in narrow, brown, felt-like panicles. There is also a white form. The flowering period of this shrub often extends to the end of September.

By carefully selecting a number of varieties it is possible to have a display of attractive white, pink and red flowers for many months. It should be stressed, however, that the beauty of the Spiraea is to be seen at its best when well-grown plants are grown singly. Most suitable for this purpose are the early, white-flowering varieties such as *S. arguta* x *vanhouttei* whose effect lies in its wealth of flowers, which often appear much earlier than other kinds of shrubs. Summer-flowering varieties, on the other hand, are more suitable for planting in bold groups among other types of shrubs. Spiraeas are also effective when planted near water or in rows, forming an attractive hedge which is sometimes cut, but more often left to grow freely. Dwarf varieties such as the Japanese *S. bullata*, *S. bumalda* 'Nyewoods', *S. pectinata*, and others are most decorative in rock-gardens.

Spiraea pruhoniciana ZEM.   Pruhonice Spiraea

This is a summer-flowering (*S. japonica* var. *ovalifolia* x *S. bumalda* 'Anthony Waterer'). It acquired its name from the place of its origin (Pruhonice, the well-known Sylva Tarrouca Park, near Prague, now a botanical garden). The hybrid was raised in 1913. It is a compact shrub about 24 inches high with large umbels of bright pink flowers with darker centres. The mass of flowers covers the green leaves which turn red in the autumn. It is effective when planted in larger compact groups in an island bed surrounded by lawns or beside paths.

Syringa   Lilac

The name of this genus comes from the Greek word 'syrinx' which means a shepherd's flute fashioned from hollow twigs. The name is of more recent origin and is not exactly fitting as the lilac has no hollow stems. The original name of 'Syringa' was, in fact, applied to *Philadelphus*. Other national names (English, French, Portuguese, Hungarian, Croatian, and others) derived from the Syrian name of this shrub — 'lelak' — are far more suitable. The first lilacs reached Europe through Busbecq, from Constantinople to Vienna.

Lilacs are native to Asia and south-east Europe. As a whole, the genus comprises about 28 species, some of which have been cultivated in the East for many generations and arrived in Europe as cultivated shrubs. They are deciduous shrubs or smaller trees which attain a height of about 30 feet, often less. The leaves are simple, rarely composite. The panicles of bloom appear on the previous year's branches, each flower consisting of a small, 4-lobed, persistent calyx and a corolla whose petals form a long tube with 2 stamens. The fruit is a capsule.

Lilac may be propagated by means of seeds which are stratified in the autumn and sown in the spring and placed in a cold-frame. Several Chinese species are easily propagated by means of summer cuttings. Hybrids are grafted onto seedling stock of *S. vulgaris* or of *Ligustrum vulgare* (Common Privet). In the latter case the grafted plant must be planted deep enough for the scion subsequently to take root.

Lilacs are hungry shrubs and should be planted in fertile, rather heavy loam, moist but well-drained. They like full sunlight but may be grown in partial shade. When planted in shade, however, they tend to produce far fewer flowers and often develop long sterile shoots. They are very hardy and do not require any protection in the winter months.

Syringa vulgaris L.   Common Lilac

This species has the form of a shrub or small tree up to 20 feet in height. It appears to have come from the Near East, having grown wild in south-east Europe for generations. It is cultivated in innumerable garden varieties, both single and double, varying from pure white to dark mauve and deep red.

Lilacs are very popular in parks and gardens. They are planted singly, in groups, and in rows to form a screen.

The tops of Lilac shrubs are inclined to become too thick and therefore it is necessary to prune them. This must be done carefully, however, by thinning out the weaker growths immediately after flowering. It is advisable to remove withered flower-heads before they start to seed.

The first Lilac shrub reached western Europe in 1566, spreading from Vienna over the rest of the Continent. In the British Isles it was first mentioned at Kew Gardens in 1597, most likely in the form of *S. vulgaris* (Common Lilac), which at that time was already widely cultivated in the Near East, and spread also in its wild form as far as south-east Europe. The Persian Lilac *S. persica,* also widely cultivated in the East, is known only in its wild form, its place of origin probably being West China. Another species well known in Europe is *S. josikaea* (Hungarian Lilac) which was discovered about 1830 by Baroness Josika at Marmarosh. This has deep lilac flowers and large glossy leaves, hairy in the early stage. It flowers in June and July. It was first discovered in a garden in cultivated form and only later in its wild state.

Plant-breeders became interested in the Lilac about 1777 when the French horticulturist Varin of Rouen crossed *S. persica* with *S. vulgaris.* Varin called this hybrid the 'Chinese Lilac', and it is now known as *S. chinensis* (syn. *S. rothomagensis*). It is commonly called the 'Rouen Lilac'. The hybrid aroused great attention with its large but somewhat sparse branches and its beautiful purple blossom. It became a parent of white, lilac-red, pink and other coloured hybrids. An important event was the discovery by the French nurseryman Lemoine of Nancy, in 1878, of a double Lilac in a private garden in Luxemburg. This variety originated as a chance mutation and was conspicuous for the size of its blooms, all earlier semi-double varieties having had only small,

Syringa vulgaris L. 'Madame Lemoine'

This hybrid is widely grown and popular for its double white blossom. It is a good variety for forcing under glass.

118

Syringa — *continued*

imperfectly shaped flowers. Following this, numerous new varieties were raised starting with 'Mathieu de Dombaste' in 1882, with beautiful mauve blossom. This was followed in 1887 by a variety known as 'Mme Jules Finger' of a pale lilac colour, and 'Senateur Volland' which opened red, becoming mauve later. In the following year the double red 'La Tour d'Auvergne' and 'Leon Simon' with bluish-pink blossoms were bred.

Another line in the cultivation of Lilacs is represented by the so-called *S.* x *hyacinthaflora* (Early Lilac) hybrids. These are hybrids obtained from *S. oblata* — which comes from northern China and has pale to purplish lilac blooms — and *S. vulgaris*. These varieties flower about 8 to 10 days earlier than other hybrids obtained from *S. vulgaris*. The individual flowers and whole panicle are quite large and their corollas do not fall after the flowering period. The colour of the flowers is usually less concentrated. Named hybrids of these early-flowering Lilacs are 'Montesquieu', purple; 'Catinat', pinkish-lilac; and 'Buffon' with lilac-pink flowers.

The Manchurian *S. amurense* has the form of a small tree. Its small strongly scented creamy-yellow flowers grow in June in panicles 4 to 6 inches long.

From central China comes *S. reflexa* which has the form of a wide shrub about 10 to 12 feet high with deep pink flowers in drooping panicles about 8 inches long in June. The buds are crimson. It is quite distinct from other Lilacs and has large leaves up to 8 inches long.

Lilacs are not only widely used in gardens, but also for floral decorations. They began to be used for the latter purpose in the second half of last century when a horticulturist at Vaugivard near Paris discovered that the natural period of winter rest of the Lilac could be considerably shortened by artificial means. Since then the practice of forcing Lilacs into flower in heated greenhouses has spread widely. Lilacs are now used in many countries for indoor decoration in the winter and early spring.

Syringa prestoniae McKELLY

This is a comparatively new hybrid race (*S. reflexa* x *S. villosa*) raised by Miss Preston at Ottawa, Canada. The original cross was made in 1920 and some 300 seedlings were raised and flowered in 1924. From the best of these the race has been propagated. They are hardy, quick-growing shrubs with graceful panicles similar to *S. reflexa* and leaves similar to *S. villosa*. Named varieties include 'Bellicent', a fragrant clear rose, 'Hiawatha', reddish-purple and 'Isabella', named after Miss Preston, which has large upright purple panicles. Miss Preston also crossed *S. reflexa* with *S. josikae* to produce a handsome race known as *S.* x *josiflexa* with fragrant panicles in June, mainly in pleasing shades of pink.

Viburnum L.   Viburnum

The origin of the name of this shrub is not quite clear. It is possible that it was derived from the Latin word 'vimen' meaning wand or from the Latin word 'viere' meaning bound. It is interesting that the English nomenclature does not include a common name for the genus. Local names usually indicate only a single variety (sometimes one variety is known by several names) and also differ considerably, obviously covering a wide variety of types, for example, Deckmanie, Hobble Bush, Appalachian Tea, White Rod, Arrow Wood, Wayfaring Tree, Nannyberry, Sheepberry, Chinese Snowball, Smooth White Rod, European Cranberrybush, Guelder Rose, Black Bow, Stag Bush, and others.

The genus comprises about 120 species which are spread in the northern temperate zone as well as in South America and Java. They are shrubs or small trees, deciduous or evergreen, leaves opposite with smooth-edged, serrated or lobed blades. The flowers are usually small, white or pinkish, in composite umbels. They consist of a 5-lobed calyx, a bell-or funnel-shaped corolla, 5 stamens, and a single seed-vessel which ripens into a drupe.

Good deep moist loamy soil is best for their successful cultivation. They are not averse to chalky soil and can withstand semi-shade, but grow better in a sunny position.

Propagation from seeds is a long process as they often do not germinate for up to 2 years. Cuttings of half-ripe wood can be taken during the summer and placed in a propagating frame. The cuttings are best taken with a heel. Rarer varieties are sometimes grafted onto *V. lantana* stock. Layering may be done in June. They are usually planted as specimens to achieve the most pleasing results. They are free-flowering although not brightly coloured. Some are outstanding in the autumn with their coloured berries and foliage.

Very popular in gardens is the Golden Rose, *V. opulus,* and particularly the variety 'Sterile', known as the Snowball Tree. Some varieties flower very early in the spring; *V. fragrans* even flowers during the winter long before its leaves appear. Another fragrant variety is *V. carlesii* illustrated in the coloured plate.

Viburnum carlesii HEMSL.   Korean Viburnum

Named after William Richard Charles, a British vice-consul in Korea who was an enthusiastic plant collector. He discovered this shrub on one of his journeys and it first flowered in England in 1906. The round clusters of flowers, which are pink in the bud stage, appear in April and May, opening to pure white. They are sweetly fragrant. Flowering is early so it is best to plant where there is protection from east winds and from the early morning sun, which can be most damaging to the flowers after a frosty night. Approximate height 5 feet.

Weigela THUNB.   Bush Honeysuckle

The Swedish botanist Thunberg named this genus after the German physician and botanist C. E. von Weigel of Greiswald. It is a small genus comprising about 12 deciduous species widely distributed in East Asia, closely related to the North American genus *Diervilla* (3 species) and often being described as a single genus under one or the other name.

Weigelas are mainly low-growing shrubs of compact, leafy growth. The leaves are opposite and are of simple, elliptical, serrated shape. The flowers are single or in clusters on short side shoots on 2-year-old branches; they are quinary, with a tubular to funnel-shaped corolla which is, compared with the Diervillas, almost regular, rarely slightly labiate. The yellow, white, red, pink to lilac, or purple flowers appear in May and June. The calyx consists of 5 sepals and the flower contains 4 stamens. The two-part seed-vessel ripens into a longish capsule.

Weigelas may be increased by seed or vegetatively. Seed should be sown in March and placed in a cold-frame. Cuttings are taken in June or July of half-ripe wood and planted in sandy soil in a propagating frame. Hard-wood cuttings taken in October and November will root in a cold-frame. Weigelas are not difficult as regards soil, although before planting the soil should be well dug and enriched with leaf-mould or peat if it is on the light side. Choose a sunny or only partly shady position, not too exposed to prevailing wind. They are hardy shrubs and when planted in suitable places do not require any protection against frost. Immediately after flowering cut out any old, dead or withered branches, and shoots which spoil the shape of the shrub.

Weigela venusta   Pink Weigela

This is a shrub some 7 feet high which originated in northern China and Korea. Its long, funnel-shaped flowers, pinkish-purple in colour, are borne in thick clusters on the arching to pendulous branches. It is very hardy. Also known as *W. florida* var. *venusta*.

124

Weigela — *continued*

Weigelas are effective when planted singly or in small groups with other low shrubs, particularly with white-flowering Spiraeas and Deutzias. They stand out especially well when planted near water, in formal pools and quiet streams. In such cases Irises of various garden forms, Astilbes, and Primulas should be planted in the foreground.

In gardens Weigelas stand out well with their slightly arching branches and conspicuous flowers which are mostly in shades of red. Exceptions are the sulphur-yellow *W. middendorffiana* which comes from Manchuria and requires a moist, protected position and partial shade and *W. maximowiczii* which comes from Japan.

The French nurseryman Lemoine raised many colourful hybrids, mostly obtained from crossing the Chinese W. *florida* and the Japanese *W. coraeensis*. The following varieties have proved very popular: 'Abel Cariere', deep rose, 'Avantgarde' with flaming red flowers, 'Conquête' with large pink flowers, the free-flowering 'Eva Rathke' with deep crimson flowers, and the new 'Newport Red'.

Of the Japanese species *W. japonica* is frequently grown in gardens and parks. It is a shrub about 7 feet high whose flowers open whitish, turning carmine later. A frequently cultivated species is *W. floribunda*, also from Japan, which attains a height of up to 8 feet with dark crimson flowers.

Weigela styriaca

This is presumed to be a hybrid of *W. coraeensis*. The shrub attains some 10 feet in height. The bright red flower clusters are in cymes containing as many as 12 blooms about 1 to $1\frac{1}{2}$ inches across, almost regular in shape, with a wide corolla suddenly narrowing into a funnel. It is a popular specimen shrub in gardens.

INDEX